# THE
# NEAREST

## Devotion Not Devotions

WHAT PEOPLE ARE SAYING ABOUT

# THE NEAREST

*What a refreshing book! If you struggle with your "devotional life" (those who don't will probably lie about other things) you are in for a wonderful surprise. With profound Biblical insight, freshness, clarity, humor and practical help, Tim Ross has given the church a magnificent gift. You will find teaching here that will revolutionize the way you think about God and your walk with him. This book could change your life! Read it and give it to your friends. They will "rise up and call you blessed" ... and you will do the same for me for having recommended it to you.*

**Professor Steve Brown**, Professor of Preaching at Reformed Theological Seminary in Orlando, Florida; the author of several books and a teacher on the radio program Key Life.

*Tim Ross has successfully and entertainingly opened up a discussion that is long overdue. This can only benefit a church that is too often ridiculously nervous about examining the truth about what actually happens to people.*

**Adrian Plass**, Writer and speaker with over thirty books to his name.

# THE
# NEAREST

## Devotion Not Devotions

## Tim Ross

Circle Books

Winchester, UK
Washington, USA

First published by Circle Books, 2011
Circle Books is an imprint of John Hunt Publishing Ltd., Laurel House, Station Approach,
Alresford, Hants, SO24 9JH, UK
office1@o-books.net
www.o-books.com

For distributor details and how to order please visit the 'Ordering' section on our website.

ISBN: 978 1 84694 508 3

A CIP catalogue record for this book is available from the British Library.

Design: Stuart Davies

Printed in the United States of America, by Edwards Brothers, Inc.

We operate a distinctive and ethical publishing philosophy in all
areas of our business, from our global network of authors to
production and worldwide distribution.

# CONTENTS

# AN ADMISSION

I don't have a quiet-time.

(Excuse me a minute while I look out of the window... No, I can't see any darkening clouds, or lightning bolts heading my way. Not yet any way.)

Personally speaking, I have always found that trying to have that regular daily devotional God-slot that people call "The Quiet-time" a great hindrance in my relationship with God. It took a few years of struggling with different times, formats and devotional aids to realise that. It has taken even longer to think and pray about what devotion really means.

When I went to theological college in training for ministry I mentioned my dilemma to other students, asked one or two of the teaching staff about it, and searched through the college library, but everyone I spoke to and everything I read began with the assumption that Christian spirituality begins with a time-slot set aside each day for personal prayer. I remember being regarded with a little suspicion when I mentioned my predicament. After all, questioning the place of private prayer is one of the few taboos in Christianity.

Being alone with God for a short period every day is regarded as a foundation stone upon which the rest of our relationship with God sits. When it comes to spirituality, the approach to and the expression of your faith in God, first and foremost, it is simply assumed that you will have some kind of private prayer time alone with God every day. The only point of discussion was what you do in that time. Yet, there I was, still struggling to lay that foundation stone. I just couldn't get the wretched thing set properly in my life. Whatever I did with it, it was always wonky. To stretch the analogy further, I wondered whether I was using the wrong cement... until I began to question whether I had the right stone in the first place.

I understood very well the place and importance of a personal relationship with God, but the only available pattern for nurturing this was the practice of slotting God into blocks of time allocated for this purpose. It felt like I was saying to God, "Ok God, this is my spiritual part of the day, this is your one chance to talk to me... what are you going to say?"

That prayer time could be used in any number of ways according to ones individual spiritual inclination or theology; with daily Bible notes, gazing at icons, saying a rosary or some other set form of prayer, but essentially, they all boiled down to the same thing. You were expected to have period of time each day in which you were 'spiritual'. That was where you got in touch with God before going out into the unspiritual world.

For a variety of reasons, some of which I will try to explain, having a worthwhile quiet-time or daily devotions was the one thing that I had found the most difficult, and sometimes just plain impossible to perform. At first, as I worked my way through the guilt brought on by countless sermons (and books) on the importance of daily devotions, I wondered why this should be. What was so wrong with me that I should find a daily quiet-time such a difficult duty to perform? Sometime later, as I started thinking about it a little more rationally, I began to wonder where the idea of a daily God-slot had arisen from in the first place, and then, more importantly, whether there were any other ways of expressing personal spirituality.

This book, then, is not intended to be an academic and theological exploration of the problem. For one thing, I am not really equipped or qualified to do that. It is intended for you, to help you if, like me, you have or want to discover a closeness with God, but for whatever reason find the traditional daily-devotional quiet time either unfulfilling, impractical or impossible.

By showing where and how I believe the quiet time came into being, and by looking at some of the underlying principles and common teachings regarding it, I hope to explode a few of the myths surrounding personal spirituality, and to give you a real sense of the assurance of God with you.

It is a partly biographical retelling of a personal search for a real and meaningful way to express my love for God, and how that search has led to the discovery of a new spirituality.

I have no illusions about this. I don't pretend to have invented anything original; it is simply new for me. It is helping me to find a freedom in living, loving and knowing God, something which struggling to have a daily quiet-time never gave.

I also realise that I am a fairly average sort of a person and therefore I am not likely to be the only one experiencing the struggles and questions that I will mention. Hopefully, if you identify yourself in what follows, you will feel less alone, and may even find some help.

You may be one of the many Christians for whom devotions have become a heavy chain. Prayer has turned into a task that holds you back in your relationship with God. You don't see devotion anymore, only devotions. You don't see love any more, only duty. On the other hand, you may be one of those for whom devotion has slipped into habit, where it is easier to love duty than it is to love God. What I want to do in this book is to show you how close God is to you, to find freedom in loving God and to know, once again, that he is with you in all things. The key is simply changing the way we understand God, or rather, the key is getting a clearer understanding of God.

There is one thing that I want to make very clear before I do go on. This book is *not* a treatise that advocates abolishing daily devotions, but it will hopefully show you that devotion is so much more than devotions. It is really an attempt to broaden our understanding of what personal prayer is. If you find having a regular quiet-time a fulfilling and meaningful act, then you should stay with it and perhaps this book may even enrich and deepen them. If, however, you find them to be lacking or missing their intended mark in your life, I hope you will find some encouragement in what follows.

## CHAPTER I

# THE NEAREST

It was a quiet day on the cloud. After listening to the angelic choir's rendition of the Hallelujah Chorus, God shifted slightly on The Mighty Golden Throne of Magnificence. He pushed his long, flowing white beard to one side, arranged the folds of his white robe in a suitably imposing manner, and peered down at earth. Far below, he could see the antlike human race scurrying about its daily business. "My creation," He mused to himself, "To do with as I please." He thought for a moment, "There must be someone down there who deserves a thunderbolt or two."

This is the stereotyped cartoon image of God that many of us, including me, grew up with. Not coming from a churchgoing family, my mental picture of God was formed by secular society's image of "The Almighty". On film, television, in the comics I read and from other atheists it was quite clear to me that God, if he existed, was a fearsome, whitebearded old man.

If the rumours about him were true, he appeared to be in a distinctly bad mood much of the time, and this ill temper had something to do with certain naughty deeds humans were doing. The consequence of this petulant pique is that occasionally God 'loses it' and sets off a volcano here or causes a hurricane there. In fact, it was not too much of a stretch to blame any or all natural disasters on the whim of the hand of God.

As I understood it, the location of this God, if he existed (which I strongly doubted) was "up there". Where "there" was, was difficult to pin down, precisely. It could be just beyond the atmosphere, albeit in some non-corporeal and therefore invisible state, or he might be even more remote, outside the universe itself. And there, high and lifted up, he remains for the most part above our lowly human affairs. Except, of course, for those occasions when he makes known his disapproval of us, and we suffer as a result.

It is still a very common idea. You could almost call it the popular secular theology of God in Western society today.

It is also a very old idea.

In ancient times the concept of God was that he was seated quite literally on a throne above the sky, which was also regarded as the limit of the cosmos itself. The sky was thought of as a sort of shell around creation outside of which was God's abode. There he sat, watching over the world, like a sort of benevolent pet owner gazing into a goldfish bowl.

It seems a reasonable enough notion; after all, surely he can only really be The Creator if he is actually greater than The Creation. For the contemporary Christian, living in a world where science is continually extending the boundaries of our knowledge of the cosmos, this puts God a very long way off indeed. Reaching inconceivable billions of miles beyond the limits of human vision and probing whole universes within atoms, astronomy and physics have made our goldfish bowl infinitely bigger with the result that there is a strong feeling in the subconscious of the agnostic and possibly even the Christian mind, of remoteness from God. In order for him to be greater than this spectacularly huge universe, he must be a very distant being indeed.

If God is there at all, he is not just above the clouds, looking in, he must be beyond the stars, and now that we know that time and space are interwoven in the fabric of the universe, he must be outside of time too. Add to this the perception that science has probed many of the questions about where life and the cosmos came from, that God, if he is greater than the sum of our knowledge, must be a radically different kind of being to us altogether.

It is almost as if, in some way, he is the furthest possible thing from us.

It is, I feel, the prevalent popular atheist or agnostic view of what God is like. It was certainly the picture I felt Christians were painting of God before I became a Christian. The entire universe is there outside our world, stretching away beyond the limits of all human knowledge and exploration; outside and greater than all this is God.

After I became a Christian, I discovered that Christian scholars tidy the idea up a bit. I learned that they talk about God as being transcendent, and say that, whatever the universe consists of, God, in order to be God, must be Other than that.

It is a concept that, if taken on its own, creates in us a deep impression that God is an extremely remote and alien being. If the only quality of God you use to approach the idea of God is this Otherness, then not only will God be greater than everything you know, he will also be different to everything you know. How then, is it possible to even consider any kind of meaningful, much less intimate, relationship with such a being? If God is so transcendent, what we can we possibly have in common?

I am not about to throw the greatness and majesty of God out of the window in favour of a pocket-sized deity. In fact I firmly believe that it is fundamentally important to spirituality to acknowledge God as being majestic and awe inspiring. To understand him as anything less is to limit him. But there are so many other qualities to God and these qualify the way we engage with his transcendence. Our problem is that we tend to take this concept and understand it in a very spatial way.

Before we redress the balance a little, a brief look at a few of the hymns that we sing affirms this common picture of a distant God: "Immortal invisible, God only wise, in light inaccessible hid from our eyes"; "O heavenly King look down from above";

"O worship the King, all glorious above"; "With gladness we worship, rejoice as we sing... The old thankful story shall scale thine abode." All emphasize the remoteness of God and reinforce this deep-rooted sense we have of his distance from us. Not only is God hidden above in some invisible realm, he is inaccessible. What is the point of even attempting to have a relationship with him? It's no wonder that the idea of God having an intimate role in our lives is one that not only non-Christians, but many churchgoers find difficult to grasp.

The perception of the remoteness of God is, as I said, not just a contemporary idea. It's one which has strong associations with the Old Testament. (I hope to show that this not the whole view of the Old Testament.) This is the God the Israelites encountered when they came to Mount Sinai after having crossed the Red Sea. Here was a God who descended (from his remote throne above); who came down upon the mountain, but whose glory had to be shrouded in a dense cloud, his people kept at a distance, behind a fence, under threat of being shot with arrows or stoned (Ex 19:9-13).

This is a God whose splendour and radiance must be shrouded from us lest it destroy us in its purity. He is an unreachable and untouchable God who must be kept further than an arm's length away. This is the picture of God we associate with the Old Testament.

The thing is, these stories were not primarily meant to illustrate God's distance from his people on earth; it is his holiness that is the central point. The idea being that because God is holy and people are not, they cannot meet on intimate terms because the result would be rather like a meeting between matter and anti-matter – annihilation.

It's a popular picture of God, both with agnostics and the kind of Christians who like to keep their religion firmly locked behind the church doors once the Sunday services are over. The reason for this is that it keeps God at a harmless and comfortable distance from us, with very little input into our lives at all. If God is so inaccessible, then all we need do is appease him with our attendance at church, or with vague belief and what we hope are the right kind of good works, and maybe that'll keep the earthquakes and hurricanes at bay.

Such a God can safely be kept to the backwaters of human life, where he is no real bother to anyone. We have even invented clichés to reinforce this: "Religion is a private thing" people say, as if we keep God at home in cupboard to be got out on rainy days when there's nothing else to do. And whenever Christian leaders put pressure on governments for social change, you know that someone is bound to say: "Religion and politics don't mix," meaning God has no place or purpose in political affairs, he is just a hobby some people do on Sundays.

In the Church this transcendent understanding of God has imparted a very distinctive colour to the whole way that we express our devotion to God. Its shades are found again and again throughout teaching about prayer and spirituality and the way we develop our relationship with him. We have learnt them so well, we don't even think about them, they are just assumed.

For one thing, when God is understood as distant, different and shrouded in mysterious splendour, he must be treated as such. As a result, our concepts of devotion and worship are subsequently coloured to sympathise with these ideas and tend to emphasise his grandeur and reverence. Our relationship to him reflects the way a servant surrenders to the will of an unseen, but great and powerful master.

St Anselm wrote this prayer, which captures something of this feeling for a transcendent God:

"O Supreme O supreme and unapproachable light, O holy and blessed Trinity, how far Thou art from me who am so near to Thee! How far art Thou removed from my vision, although I am so near to Thine! Everywhere Thou art wholly

present and I see Thee not. In Thee I move and in Thee I have my being and cannot come to Thee."
Proslogium, chapter 16.

But Jesus shows us a different pattern.

When it comes to prayer, he teaches us to call God "Our Father". God is in heaven and his will must be done, but he is not a master issuing orders to his minions. His attitude to us is first and foremost parental. This great and mighty God, who holds the universe in the palm of his hand, who speaks and life is created, wants to treat us as his children, and he wants us to treat him as our Father.

And in Jesus, we see something even more wonderful.

In Jesus we see this great, distant unknowable God coming down from the mountain, through the clouds to us, to be with us, to be close to us, to be knowable and touchable. In Jesus the Unreachable and Unknowable reaches out to touch. That is incarnation, God taking part in every human experience, God coming into my experience with me.

As far as spirituality goes, the most important Christian doctrine of all is incarnation, because it gives us the focal point for our conversation with God. Like one of those giant radio telescopes pointing out into space, searching for its target in the faintest echoes across the reaches of space and then finding instead that what we have been looking for is actually here on earth. That is the kind of radical change of direction, shift in our thinking and transformation of our perception of God that the incarnation requires of us.

Understanding incarnation changes the whole direction and manner of our devotion, because it means that in Jesus, God is here.

In Jesus, God is Emmanuel, God with us. He is no longer anywhere else; he is not *there* anymore but *here*. He is not the furthest anymore, he is The Nearest.

What if you begin with that? What if you strip everything else away, assume nothing, and let that one thought shape the way you think about how you express your relationship with God?

*****

Jesus is the Nearest. In Jesus, God comes to ordinary human life - to every part of it: the tax office, the market, the local baths and wedding receptions. God is here and he is not here merely as an impartial observer to your activities, or even just to police them. He is here to make a difference... here. In Jesus the unreachable and untouchable reaches out to touch. In Jesus, God comes to your here, to be with you in whatever and wherever your here might be, from one moment to the next.

When you find yourself tired with the stresses of life and so drained that you feel you do not even have the spiritual or physical energy to come to God in prayer; that is your Here, and God is here. When you feel isolated in pain or suffering, cut off from any human understanding of where you are and how you feel; that is your Here, and God is here. When you feel spiritually dried up, with nothing left to give God, or that you have let him down yet again; _that_ is your Here, and God is here with you.

Your Here is your now. Whether it is something as mundane as peeling today's vegetables, or being at work, or whether it is in times of extreme emotion. God is always here.

In all things and in all of life, God is The Nearest; and because he is The Nearest he is not anywhere else. To understand that is to find Freedom and Life because it means that you no longer need to go anywhere else to meet him. You no longer have to drag yourself out of your now in order to go and find him in some artificially created spiritual mood. He is not _there_ anymore; he is always here, The Nearest.

I am beginning to learn this lesson, that God is the Nearest for me, but it has not always been that way. I became a Christian at the age of eighteen. From being a firm, almost ardent atheist, my life was turned around one night when I met Jesus in the kitchen of some Christian friends. We were doing the washing up, and you can't get much more mundane than that.

The first few months of my Christian life were probably the nearest I shall ever get to feeling weightless. I had been suddenly confronted with the reality of God's existence in a way I could no longer deny. I felt overwhelmed, lifted and wonderfully embraced and accepted by a very powerful kind of love. It was like a spiritual magic carpet that carried me about on air.

The feeling didn't last forever, though. After a few months, the magic carpet landed and I went through a period where I felt as if I was falling further and further away from God. There was nothing I could do to stop it. It was as if God had knocked away all the supports with which I propped up my life and, without them, I fell down a deep dark hole.

But I didn't stop falling, I kept going down, further and further away from God, and then it was like falling through the bottom of that hole. From where I stood, it felt as if God was unimaginably far away. The distance from him was greater than I felt I could bear and there seemed to be nothing that I could do to get out of the hole. I felt something of the anguish of the Psalmist when he cried out, "Why are you so far from saving me, so far from the words of my groanings? O my God, I cry out by day, but you do not answer" (Psalm 22:1,2).

There was no great flash of revelation that spirited me out of the hole, no miraculous turn around, as there had been at my conversion. Instead, it was a gradual climb, as the Lord began the work of re-shaping my understanding of what he is really like.

As sometimes happens at times like this, various passages from the Bible stick out and become helpful or encouraging. That was so for me. A few passages and verses became especially meaningful at that time, but none more so than Psalm 139.

Even though I had read them before, verses 7-11 of the Psalm took on a whole new meaning and shone a flicker of light into my distress:

> "Where can I go from your Spirit? Where can I flee from your presence? If I go up to the heavens, you are there;
> If I make my bed in the depths, you are there. If I rise on the wings of the dawn, if I settle on the far side of the sea, even there your hand will guide me, your right hand will hold me fast. If I say, 'Surely the darkness will hide me and the light become night around me,' Even the darkness will not be dark to you; the night will shine like the day, for darkness is as light to you."

This was the first and most important lesson I had to learn. Whilst I was still sitting at the bottom of the hole, and before I even thought about trying to climb out, I needed to be shown that I didn't have to haul myself out of the hole to find God again.

The Psalm spelled it out so clearly. He was with me there in the hole. I had known him briefly in the heights, but that was a first "honeymoon" experience of God. Now he wanted me to know that he was with me "in the depths."

In the darkness of my hole, God was there.

With an enormous sense of relief I realised that it was not up to me to claw my way out of the hole, he had come to me. Or rather, he had always been with me, there in the hole.

That was what I had to understand, and that is the Gospel, the incarnation. It is God moving to us, not us to God. To understand that is to understand the purpose of the incarnation and the cross. God comes into our depths, so that we might find and know him here, and to save us here. We haven't got to move one inch from where we are in order to meet him, ever.

From my perspective, it was as if the whole purpose of Jesus' coming to earth was to come and meet me in my hole, not to take me out of it to meet God, but to bring him into it.

That was the first new understanding for me; the second new understanding came later. As I began to accept with increasing assurance that God was with me, I started to realise, from verse 1-4 of Psalm 139, just how close God was.

"O Lord, you have searched me and you know me. You know when I sit and when I rise; you perceive my thoughts from afar. You discern my going out and my lying down; you are familiar with all my ways. Before a word is on my tongue you know it completely, O Lord."

Reading that last line one day, I was hit with a thought that really was like a flash of lightning. When the writer says, "Before a word is on my tongue you know it completely," he is not really saying that God knows what you are going to say because he can see into the future. Look at the line before, "You are familiar with all my ways." He is saying that God knows you so intimately he knows exactly how you think. That is how he knows what you are going to say, because, like the most intimate and attentive of lovers, all your ways are completely familiar to him.

God is close to you. Nearer even than your next thought.

Put those two flashes of light together, God is with you in whatever situation you find yourself and he knows you intimately and completely, and you have an extremely powerful foundation for true spiritual strength.

When the Psalmist wrote, "Where can I go from your Spirit? Where can I flee from your presence?" he wasn't finally caving in and accepting the presence of God in his life, he was exulting in the joyful liberation that comes from knowing that there is absolutely no situation in life where he will find that God is absent.

He knows you, the you that is deep inside. He searches the depths of your being with his presence. You breathe without thinking and yet he is nearer even than your next breath.

So close is he to you that you do not have to move at all to find him. In fact you must not move, because he is here with you exactly as you are. If you try to change anything because of expectations you think you have to match in order to meet God, then often it will be those expectations that you will meet, not him.

Take hold of these two thoughts, embrace them and absorb them, and they will change your whole understanding of what prayer is all about.

God is with you always, closer than you can ever imagine. He is always at the edge of conscious thought. It's such a simple and obvious truth, but if you begin to reconstruct your idea of what spirituality is all about from this one point, it is life transforming, because it implies two things.

The first implication seems, at first glance, to count against the idea of approaching devotion from this point of view. If God is immediately close to your inmost thoughts, there is a real danger of making him convenient. A prayer of the heart is now no more than a thought away so you can easily be tempted to turn to him only when you need him, and then to forget his presence when you don't. Worse still, it is even easier to quietly ignore him. At least if you force yourself to sit through the routine of a daily quiet time, you are forced to consider the idea of God if nothing else. However a still, small voice can so easily be drowned out by thunder and earthquakes of your own making, and you must accept that that will happen, if you take this as your model for spirituality. But you know what? God knows that about you too. He knows what human nature is like, he designed us! So he is closer to us even during what we think of as a failure.

The second consequence of God being so close to the inmost thoughts of your heart is immediately more positive. If you accept that God is The Nearest in any and every circumstance of life, and if you accept the discipline of developing the habit of turning to him wherever you are and in whatever you do, immediately God becomes a part of all that you are and all that you do.

The growing consciousness of his inescapable presence makes your subconscious reasons for keeping him at bay begin to lose their power. His presence becomes less a convenient service to be called upon as required and more the essential part of your life.

He is nearer than your next thought and never any further away than that. You need only turn your thoughts to him and he is here. This is not to say that you forget altogether that God, who is here, who is the Nearest, is also the Creator of all that is. If you do, you make him less than God and you lose the purpose of his presence – which is to hold and sustain you. He is present not just to be a companionable friend through life, he is present Here to make a difference Here. He can do that because he is the creator of everything that exists.

Only his presence, in this world and in our lives can make the difference that is needed. We need both a transcendent and an incarnate God. We need an unimaginably great, limitlessly powerful, and inexpressibly loving being... but we need him here with us. You need that God close to you, as a part of all your life's intricacies. Psalm 139 describes how God is both.

God is The Nearest. In discovering this, I have discovered that I need an approach to spirituality which reflects this. In struggling and not always succeeding with the traditional, daily quiet-time model for spirituality I have found that I need a devotional model which seeks closeness with God in all of life.

This is radically different to an understanding of prayer in which we feel we have to try and scale some mountain, penetrate some cloud or cut ourselves off from the world in order to meet God. Instead we try to develop an awareness of God in life; to meet him in our Here, and talk with him in whatever Here we find ourselves in.

The world touches our lives in so many different ways. Its problems, pressures and pains all are near to us. Sometimes they are closer than at others, and sometimes they are so near our lives are affected drastically, yet God is nearer still.

He is nearer than anything else. Nearer even than the sin you sometimes feel comes between you and God. You might think that your actions have created a barrier between you and God, but for you, as a follower of Jesus, that is just your perception. From God's point of view he is standing right there alongside you as you stare at whatever wall you think you have placed between yourself and him.

It is Psalm 193 again: There is no place in all human experience where God is absent. There is not one single place in the whole of human existence where you cannot know the holding, guiding hand of God in your life.

One thing you need to accept from the outset, however, is that you will not always experience the closeness of his presence as a tangible feeling. In fact there are likely to be times when you feel that you are at the bottom of that hole again, but he is there. There is no hard climb out of the hole, no crossing a gulf, nor is there some standard of model Christian behaviour that must be reached in order to come close to God. There is only a yearning to know God who is the Nearest.

CHAPTER 2

# THE FURTHEST

## The Origins Of The Quiet Time

God is closer and more immediate to us than anything without or within.

There is one, simple fact that challenges this truth, and that is that we just do not always feel that he really is present. Those times, when the intimate presence fills us and makes even thought redundant, are special oases in our pilgrimage. There are other times when we find ourselves in a desert and the reality of God seems like a distant mirage. Most of the time, we find ourselves in neither extreme. Life ticks by and God is neither powerfully present nor desolately absent.

Whether or not that is the way things should be, that is the way they are. In a way, it was like that for the disciples too. Although they did witness a tremendously dramatic ministry in the life of Jesus, the mountain top transfiguration and the perilous storm at sea were equivalent to these poles of experience. What the writers of the Gospels don't include in their writings was all the ordinary, everyday stuff that must have happened in between all the amazing events.

You never, for instance, find Matthew saying, "And on the second day of the week Simon went into Bethphage with Judas and they did purchase a loaf of bread and some marmite. And Jesus and the disciples ate bread and marmite sandwiches and chatted about nothing in particular." But it must have happened (apart from the marmite, of course). It wasn't all parables and miracles. There would have been large amounts of time when they were simply journeying with him from place to place and sharing in his work, which is not a bad way of describing the Christian life, when you think about it.

There is still the unanswered question of why should this be, though. If God is unchangeably The Nearest, why can we not feel his intense presence constantly?

The answer we usually come up with is that the fault must lie with us somewhere. "It must be my fault," we tell ourselves, "If God is constant, it must be me who is spiritually inconstant." There is a very strong voice within us that says, "*If* I were a better Christian, *if* I had more faith, *if* I gave more time to him, *if* I prayed more, *then* I might know God's presence more in my life."

Somewhere in the back of our minds we have forged a link between the sense of God's presence and how 'spiritual' a person we are. This, we tell ourselves, must be the answer as to why we don't sense his presence all the time. We're just not good enough, spiritually.

It seems like such a reasonable answer, but I am convinced that it is not the right answer. Very far from it. For one thing, can you really imagine God, whom Jesus teaches us to think of as a loving father, is really going to say to us, "I'm not going to be with you today because you're just not good enough." Or that at some point during our prayers he suddenly pops up, like Aladdin's genie, and says, "I am present now, tell me want you want so I can grant your wishes." And yet, in a very crude way, that is frequently how we are led to believe prayer works.

It is true that he wants sincerity and wholehearted commitment in your quest for a closer relationship with him. This is what is implied in Jeremiah 29:13 where God says, "You will find me, when you seek me with all your heart." This is the 'magic lamp' verse so often quoted in sermons about finding and knowing the presence of God.

If you pull out all the stops, spiritually speaking (so we are told), God will condescend to be present with you. But what you need to realise is that this is not a one-sided verse. The emphasis here is as much on the promise of him being found as it is on the call to seek him earnestly.

Who has not, after reading that, wanted to cry out, "I am seeking you, why can't I find you? What more do you want from me?" Then, because of this association between the sense of God's presence and devotional good works, we are convinced that we need to pray and read the Bible more. "Maybe if I prayed for forty-five minutes instead of thirty," you say to yourself, "And read two chapters of the Bible instead of one, perhaps then I would be more spiritual person."

It is precisely at this point that guilt frequently pops up his ugly head and says, "Hello. It's me again." With all the pressures of modern life, how can you change things to devote more time to God? And the result is that your devotion to God has now become just another stress in life.

If you want a good discussion starter for a fellowship group you, only need to ask two questions: "Who feels guilty about the adequacy of their prayer life?" and in response, "Why?"

You'll probably get one of two responses. If you have the kind of home group where people feel they can be reasonably open with each other, you will almost certainly get a few raised hands or nods of agreement. The other possibility is that you will be greeted with a guilty, stony-faced silence. You have raised a taboo that people are uncomfortable with and don't really want to face up to, because doing so, they fear, will require them to make even more commitments with their time and energy. One thing you will almost certainly discover, though, is that you are not alone, and that it is quite a common experience to feel that we do not pray enough, or that our devotional life is not what we feel it should be.

As with any stress, it helps if you face up to it, instead of avoiding it. Part of the guilt you feel is because of the perceived conflict between the demands of everyday living and the amount of time you can feasibly spend in prayer. Whatever conclusions you come to, at this point, the most important thing now is to understand that guilt should never be the basis for a truly loving relationship with anyone, much less God.

And yet, bizarre as it sounds, this guilt does actually have a plus side. It is absolute proof positive of your love for God and deep desire to know him. Recognise and accept this, and you will begin to conquer the guilt, instead of letting it dictate the way you approach prayer and devotion.

So here is the slightly weird state of affairs we are in at the moment. Jeremiah 29:13 tells us to seek God with all our heart, which results in us feeling guilty about not praying enough. Yet this guilt, when recognised for what it is, can actually make us feel a bit better about ourselves. Well, it's a start... of sorts.

Suppose we look at Jeremiah 29:13 another way. Why should we assume that where it talks about sincerity and wholehearted commitment, it's talking about our actions? I don't think it is. I think it's talking about the sincerity of your will and whole-heartedness of purpose in wanting to seek God. So when God says, "You will find me, when you seek me with all your heart," it is actually about you being wholehearted instead of half-hearted in your love and desire to find him, rather than turning over yet more of your diary to him.

In fact, I would go so far as to say that, from this point of view, is actually possible to be perfect. I'm not saying that you will never sin or make a single mistake again. I'm saying that a perfect, wholehearted desire for God is achievable in your lifetime. Though this may seem a little out of reach, it is certainly possible, probable even, that if the chief goal of your life is to seek God and love him, there will definitely be moments of perfection, where your desire for God consumes your whole will, and everything else becomes unimportant.

These moments of perfection may be transitory, but what

isn't transitory is the importance of God to you. Your innermost desire is that you want him to be number one and you want your life to reflect that inner devotion. As I've said before, the very fact that you have an inner turmoil about this is proof of your desire – if God wasn't important to you, you wouldn't be worried about the amount of time you spend with him.

Even St Paul experienced this inner warring between what he wanted in his heart and what he found himself doing in practice. In a touching moment in the book of Romans, he expresses his personal anguish. "For in my inner being I delight in God's law; but I see another law at work in the members of my body, waging war against the law of my mind and making me a prisoner... Who will rescue me from this body of death? Thanks be to God - Through Jesus Christ our Lord!" (Romans 7:22, 23 & 25). If a saint can go through this experience, it is completely normal that you should feel this way too.

Realising that you can wholeheartedly love and desire God in your inner being is a part of the answer, but it is only half of the answer because the real question that your guilt is asking is, "How much time should I give to God in prayer and devotions?" By which it means, "Precisely how much time do I need give and what do I need to do during that time so that God is honoured and the guilt is satisfied."

Unfortunately, guilt is rarely satisfied that easily. It will take as much as you want to give, and keep asking for more. What is worse, if you are not careful, you end up trying to measure your relationship with God in terms of the quantity or quality of time you give to him.

The moment you judge your relationship with God in terms of how much time you spend in prayer, or some subjective standard of spiritual activity, that is the moment your relationship ceases to be a personal one and becomes a contractual one. You are defining your relationship by spiritual duties performed. "My relationship with God will be satisfactory when I spend X amount of time in prayer, read X amount of the Bible, or incorporate X amount of spiritual activities in my life."

Jesus said, "I no longer call you servants, you are my friends..." and it is so easy to fall into the trap of taking on the role of a servant or an employee fulfilling their required duties. Go down this route and you end up chasing answers to yet more questions like: "What kind of devotions should I have?" "What shape should it take?" "What devotional books and aids should I use?" "How much time should I spend in this or that aspect of prayer?"

Although these are important questions, I found that trying to answer them took over my whole life for a couple of years as I tried to find the "right" way to have a quiet-time. As a result I have ended up with no less than seven daily devotional books, all started with good intentions but none finished.

I can also clearly remember the day when, not for the first time, I looked back through a week's worth of unread notes from one of those daily Bible booklets one can buy, and wondered how I was going find time to read them. At which point I put the uncompleted pamphlet on the pile of other half finished booklets, and then, with an intake of breath... threw the whole lot in the bin.

Over the years I tried all sorts of different methods for devotions: silent meditations, going for a walk, following set prayers etc. Nothing fitted my needs until it dawned on me that in all my seeking to know God more closely there were two further questions that I had not even considered.

It was during my training for Methodist ministry that my thoughts really crystallised. Specifically, it was during a seminar on Spirituality for the Minister. We had been looking at various models for personal devotions. They were all based upon the custom of fitting a daily God-slot into the minister's timetable. As the discussion continued and the merits of candles, prayer diaries and worship centres were considered, I felt the years of frustrated attempts at systematic quiet-times coming up to the surface.

Before I had really thought about what I was saying, the question was out, "Is the quiet-time the only model for personal devotions?"

I was greeted with blank looks and a silence which could only be described as mystified.

Inside I had the feeling that I had at last discovered the question to the answer that I had been looking for. Excitement bubbled up inside me, like effervescence released in an opened cola bottle, so I tried again, "Is having a daily quiet-time the only possible model for personal devotions?"

Again I got puzzled looks and I half wondered whether I had suddenly started speaking in tongues without realising it. No one really seemed to know just what it was I was asking. It was rather like being at a convention of bakers and asking whether using yeast and flour was the only way of making bread. The question was quickly set aside and the discussion returned to the original subject.

But it was too late, now I'd let the genie out of the bottle I couldn't keep it in. If you'll excuse me switching metaphors, it was as though I had been a dark room and someone had turned on a light. At last I could begin to see my surroundings – the next step was to make sense of them.

I felt like Archimedes in his eureka moment, only instead of running down the street naked, I wanted to bring it into every conversation. It didn't particularly matter what the subject was either: "Tim, did you see the college football match yesterday afternoon?" "No... but do you think a quiet-time is the only way for a Christian to stay close to God?"

Whoever I asked, I got the same baffled response. At first I was worried that I had a serious communication problem, a little later I realised what the problem was. To those I had asked, it was a bit like asking if a square was the only basic model for a cube, it was a non-question. All the same, the more I thought about it, the more I became convinced that this was _the_ question about spirituality, for me at least. Why was having daily devotions the only available model for Christian spirituality?

For a while, I got no further than simply framing the question until I began looking at the next question that naturally arose from it. Before I could look for other models I realised that I needed to know where the concept of daily devotions came from.

What are the roots of the quiet-time and is it really the only model for personal spirituality? Looking for the answers to these two questions has been a pilgrimage in itself. Although this journey will probably last a lifetime, I am beginning to see other dimensions to spirituality, and consequently to the Christian life, that I hadn't even considered before.

The first extremely surprising discovery I made was that what we think of as a quiet-time or daily devotions, this period of solitary prayer and Bible reading every day, is not primarily a biblical model. There is no mention of the quiet-time as a model for prayer anywhere in the Bible. It is true that Jesus went off alone at times, to be with the Father to pray, but there is no suggestion that this was a daily occurrence, or one which he recommended the disciples should do on a daily basis. He certainly never taught that private devotions were the only way to pray.

When the disciples asked Jesus to teach them his secrets of prayer in the same way other spiritual leaders taught their followers their own methods, Jesus taught them the Lord's Prayer. It's worth pointing out that when Jesus says, "When you pray, say 'Our Father...'", both the words 'you' and 'our' are plural in the language of the Greek New Testament. We assume that Jesus used the plural 'you' because he was speaking to the disciples as a group, but the additional use of the word 'our' has inspired Christians down the centuries to use this as a corporate prayer.

In Matthew's gospel, by way of an introduction to the Lord's Prayer Jesus says, "When you pray, go into your room, close the door and pray to your Father, who is unseen" (Matt 6:6) Which we usually interpret to mean, "The only way you can pray is to lock yourself away from the world for half an hour". There is no particular reason why we should assume that Jesus meant we should go into a private room, on our own. He could just as easily have been addressing this instruction to the disciples as a group. "When all of you pray, you should go into your room (together) and say, 'Our Father...'". Something most Christians do virtually every Sunday, behind closed doors in Church. Though the word 'room' also needs to be understood correctly too, something I'll come back to later.

In the Hebrew world of the Bible it was common to try to make a point by giving an example of extreme opposites. So, for instance, in Malachi 1:2, 3, God says, "I have loved Jacob, but Esau I have hated." Which does not mean that we are expected to believe God actually hated Esau, as if he were capable of hate, but that his attitude toward Jacob and Esau was so extremely different as to appear almost like opposite poles. Here, in Matthew, Jesus is using the same technique.

This is not meant primarily as a command to the individual for private prayer any more than when Jesus says, "When you pray say, 'Our Father, who art in heaven...'" he expects us only to recite the Lord's Prayer every time we pray. The context of the Lord's Prayer is Jesus' instructions about not praying on the street corners like the hypocrites. The teaching, given to the believing community (here the disciples), is primarily against praying insincerely but instead praying in the spirit of the Lord's Prayer.

The common practice, amongst Jews in Jesus' time, was to pray three times a day. This normally took place in a synagogue, but if that couldn't happen then it was done wherever one was. It is not too difficult to see how, if you wanted to be seen to be doing the right thing, you could engineer your circumstances so that you would end up in some public place at the time of prayer.

The opposite, Jesus says, is to go into your "room." The word he used here referred to an inner store room, which was perhaps a store cupboard or place to keep valuables safe. This must have been a bit of a shock to the disciples who were used to prayer being done in a religious context.

What Jesus is saying, then, is that for prayer to be a part of your ordinary everyday lives, you shouldn't be trapped into thinking of it as being some kind of ritualistic act that requires you to get into the right place, be in a particular frame of mind or use the right language. Everyday life should be the place and language of prayer.

In the book of Acts it is quite clear that the daily devotional activities that stood out in the early Church were the times they met together for prayer and fellowship. Paul's teachings on worship in passages like 1 Corinthians chapters 11-14 are aimed at these corporate acts of devotion of the Christian community. This does not mean that there was no personal devotion taking place, it just means that the first believers probably carried on with their version of what would have been the normal practice of Judaism.

In Judaism the emphasis is more about the spirituality of the community and family prayer than on the individual. The concepts of personal faith, personal salvation and personal devotion are very much Christian ideas that have evolved through the history of the Church and have been particularly emphasised in our current, distinctively individualistic society.

I don't want to go into a discussion of the rights and wrongs of that here, and I want to be very clear that I am not saying we should throw out the quiet-time and never have personal prayer. If anything, it is the opposite, because you cannot develop any relationship without communication. But I do think the place of traditional daily devotions in Christian spirituality needs to be reconsidered. What I want to do is to look at the development of the quiet-time as the mainstay of spirituality along with some the ideas that we associate with it, and ask whether it is the only appropriate way to express our love for God.

First, let's look at how I believe the practice of daily devotions came into being.

Although the early, post New Testament Christians saw themselves as belonging together in the "Body of Christ", they still struggled with the same sort of questions we struggle with about developing a strong faith and spirituality. Some felt that the problem was not just an internal one. "We struggle," they argued, "Because the world is pagan and in its fallen state it tempts us with the pleasures it offers. These distract us from our ultimate goal of a life devoted to God."

Some took this line of reasoning further and looked to the life of Jesus as a model. They saw how he wrestled to overcome temptation in the desert and reasoned that if they lived strict, simple lives, or even cut themselves off from the world, as Jesus did, they would be better able to face its temptations and concentrate more on living a truly spiritual life.

In an attempt to achieve this, a man called Cyprian, who was the Bishop of Carthage around 250 AD, put himself under vows of chastity and poverty. Other Christians followed his pattern but took Jesus' example very literally and became hermits living on the edges of the desert. Still others cut themselves off from the world in the extreme by living on pillars or walling themselves up inside caves for a while.

It was not long before some spiritual leaders, like St Anthony, who I will talk about later, found groups of followers gathering around to listen to the insights and wisdom they had gained through their spiritual struggles and encounters with God. Followers eventually became acolytes, taking up permanent residence around the leaders, whose example they followed, creating the beginnings of the first monastic communities. Later ascetics went further and deliberately set up monasteries where the community was expected to live by a common rule, built around a pattern of private prayer, common worship, study and manual work.

St Benedict of Nursia in particular, saw the need for these monastic communities to have clearly defined goals for an ordered and progressive spiritual life. From him we get the Rule of Benedict, which became a cornerstone of monastic spirituality, with its emphasis on humility interpreted as self-abasement. The scriptural basis that he took was the proclamation of Jesus that those who humble themselves will be exalted (Luke 14:11). This was understood to mean that true humility involved believing oneself to be not just lower, but actually of less worth than all others.

The monasteries grew and developed over time, eventually becoming an organised and dominant movement in the Christian Church. All had a common aim; to develop a deep devotion to Christ in as simple an environment as was possible, free from the distractions of the world. These 'distractions' have varied a bit down the ages, but broadly they centred around rich living, sexual relationships and lack of self-discipline. Consequently the vows that were taken were poverty, chastity or celibacy and obedience. In fact anything that vaguely resembled comfort or luxury was considered worldly and was viewed as detrimental to living the spiritual life. Out with soft silk garments and feathered beds, in with hair shirts and simple cots.

Over time, the monasteries grew in power, influence and wealth, and many of the great cathedrals of Europe were raised from the treasuries of monasteries. In some quarters, this led to excesses and a certain relaxation of the ascetic disciplines. Whilst it is somewhat of a stereotype, it is no accident that friars are frequently portrayed as fat on film and television. For some, this was a betrayal of the principles of monasticism. One monastic order in particular, the Cistercians, was founded to bring monasticism back to its original principles of self-denial and austerity, which they felt had been forsaken.

Cistercian monasteries and churches were very plain, stripped of excess and anything that might be associated with luxury or wealth. The Cistercians were nicknamed "White Monks" because they regarded even dyes as an extravagance and so wore only undyed wool. Women had to remain firmly outside the abbey gates along with hawks and dogs because of their association with carnal and wasteful leisure pursuits (hunting, in the case of the hawks and dogs).

Carthusian monks took this principle of alienation from the world to the extreme, valuing solitude above all else as the most praiseworthy spiritual discipline. They isolated themselves not only from the world, but also from each other. Being cloistered in a community within the walls of a monastery was not enough. Inside their monastery they lived in self-contained cottages or cells, each with its own garden from which they never emerged, except for certain offices of prayer. What food they couldn't grow and other essential supplies that they needed were passed to them through a hatch. The only human contact they were allowed were the few liturgies that they said together; the rest of life was lived in self-imposed solitary confinement.

One reason for the growth of the monasteries was the development of a branch of theology that put God at a great distance from us. In these first few centuries of the early church, there were those who believed that the world was not just imperfect; instead it was believed to be essentially evil and opposed to God. Some theologians and Church leaders taught that there was a gulf between the world and all it stood for, and God, so that the purpose of the Christian life was to cross that gulf.

Around the end of the fourth century, Augustine, the Bishop of Hippo Regius in north Africa, looked on the world as a Godless place, and was among the first to put into concrete terms the need for withdrawal and contemplation as being necessary for finding closeness with God. For Augustine, contemplative prayer, performed in solitude, was the means of leaving the world and ascending to God.

Augustine was himself influenced by the ideas of the Greek philosopher Plato, who saw the world as only a shadowy form of the true reality found in God, and believed that our purpose was to move from the shadows of this world into the light, through meditation on God's supreme beauty. John Cassian, a contemporary of Augustine's, felt that, in this respect, the hermit's life was the ideal Christian life because it made continuous contemplative prayer away from the world possible.

In the latter part of the sixth century, Gregory the Great gave up a wealthy Roman inheritance for a life of poverty and austerity. His contribution to spirituality was the idea that the Christian life is a journey in which the aim is to become detached from the world by seeking God. Gradually these ideas, together with Augustine's Christian interpretation of Platonic philosophy, gelled together into the fundamental principles of monasticism.

At first the monastic life was seen only as an alternative to the normal Christian life, but by medieval times the monasteries had grown in power and influence, and increasingly came to be seen as an ideal spiritual life. In the middle of the twelfth century, there were about seven hundred and fifty monasteries and abbeys in England, and between them they owned fifteen percent of the land in the form of farms, forests and large estates.

This meant that monasteries were big business. Large work forces of local labour were needed to work the lands and service the monasteries. Tintern Abbey, for instance, owned up to twelve farms at one stage in its life. The Abbot at Fountains Abbey in Yorkshire had a staff of four hundred lay people who worked as farm workers, launderers and butlers. Even by today's standards that is a good-sized company.

In many places the local church was either a place of worship controlled by a monastery, or the monastery itself, which was usually the centre of both the spiritual and social life of the town or village. The influence of the monasteries on theology and spirituality grew alongside their place in society. The only worship and spiritual example many people had was monasticism, such that, in time, the ascetic life was seen as the definitive and supreme way for Christians to express their devotion to God.

It is in this that we can see the beginnings of the practice of the daily devotional quiet time. Monks in those days were regarded as a sort of spiritual elite and living the ideal Christian life (perhaps they still are today). They lived by the discipline of their rule, but it was not possible for ordinary Christians to attend their numerous times of prayer throughout the day. Some were able to become "lay brothers", even having their own quarters inside or in the vicinity of the monastery. They served the monks in practical ways but had not taken the vows. Nevertheless they were able to follow the devotional pattern of the monks very closely.

For other devout believers, who were living 'normal' lives outside the monastery, the best they could do was to try to emulate the spiritual life of the monks, saying their own prayers in private and following the monk's disciplined and ascetic life as closely as was possible. The underlying theological principles remained; people are alienated from God in their worldly ways and salvation is the beginning of a journey out of the evil world to God. This journey was only achievable by first trying to shake off the world's hold on us, and this in turn could only be attained by a life of prayer and contemplation on God.

Into this historical stew, mystics and spiritual writers added other ideas. The mystics were devout Christians who sought experiences of God's actual presence. These, they also felt, could only be achieved by a life dedicated to meditation and contemplation.

Teresa of Avila, a nun writing in the middle of the sixteenth century, talked of the life of prayer as a journey to an 'Inner Castle'. John of the Cross, writing at the same time as Teresa, urged his followers to find the Dark Night of the Soul where everything that satisfies us, both physically and spiritually must be left behind. In similar vein an unknown author urged us to enter The Cloud of Unknowing, in which we leave behind all that we know of God and ascend into the unknowable depths of God's presence.

The point in illustrating this potted history is to hear the echoes of ideas that we still associate with the quiet time and to show where the contemporary understanding of the nature of prayer evolved from.

## The Key Principles Of The Quiet Time

One of the strongest, most pervasive ideas in Christian spirituality, is the idea that God's presence is most keenly felt when we draw ourselves aside from the busy-ness and clamour of the world in order to enter the presence of God.

Underlying this and the monastic approaches to prayer it came from, is the idea of movement.

There is an old evangelistic tract handed out on street corners that begins with an illustration of an enormous chasm between the human race and God. The chasm symbolises sin, which, unless it is dealt with, cannot be bridged. The chasm is really symbolic of the idea of the essential flaw in the human nature that separates humanity from God. In the tract the next image shows a cross forming a bridge over the chasm with the explanation that through the saving act of Christ we can come to God once again.

Whatever you think about the theology of this tract, the danger with the chasm idea is that it is a very spatial illustration. It gives the impression that our sins make God *actually* distant from us, or create a tangible barrier between us, which has to be bridged or removed before we can come close to him. The last part of the tract explains how a prayer of repentance is the way this chasm is crossed and our relationship with God is restored.

Forgetting all the passages in the New Testament which make clear that if we are in Christ, we have crossed the chasm and are with Christ in God, we carry over this sin=chasm idea into our Christian lives. Sin creates a gulf which must be crossed, since "If we claim to be without sin, we deceive ourselves" (1 John 1:8). It follows that personal prayer begins as an attempt to bridge the gulf once more. So, again, we are back into images of movement, and it is not too difficult to see how the idea that prayer takes us from where we are to where God is has percolated all our ideas about the purpose of spirituality.

From this perspective, prayer becomes the vehicle to carry us to God, wherever he is felt to be. Now we can see the link between mediaeval monastic spirituality and many of the ideas that we associate with the need for a quiet-time. The world in which we live is seen at the very least as something that distracts us from God, tempts us to sin, and drains our spiritual resources, or in the extreme, it is the realm of evil from which we must flee.

How often have you heard 'The Kingdom' and 'The World' used as opposites in sermons? If that is truly the case, then it seems logical that to enter one we must have to exit the other. To find God and get close to him, a Christian must first 'put the world aside,' 'leave the world behind,' 'step into the presence' etc. All of which are ideas involving movement!

Far from being The Nearest, God is almost regarded as The Furthest. We are back in the fish bowl again, straining to get a glimpse of the Great Being beyond the algae covered glass which surrounds us. In the extreme, this kind of thinking implies that the whole purpose of prayer is primarily to take us for a time out of the world's grasp, to bridge that gap between God and us, and finally make contact with the Divine.

A more common and prevailing idea, is the concept that the quiet-time is essential for our spiritual health because it enables us, for a while, to set aside the distractions and stresses of the world and focus on the reality of God. It is, in essence, going into one's own cell, in some way or other, to find God before going out again to face the world.

Whilst they are extremely valuable, Christian retreats, however short or long, can foster this same concept, of the need for movement away from the world towards God. Some of the models and images we use in talking about personal devotions reinforce this 'separate unto the Lord' feeling we have about prayer. Phrases like 'ascending the mount of prayer' and 'entering the presence or throne room of God' use pictures that directly refer to prayer in terms of movement towards this far away God. Prayer has become vehicular, a means of transport to get us *to* God.

One of the most commonly used Biblical narratives by devotional writers and leaders of quiet days is the account in Luke 10:38-42 of Mary and Martha entertaining Jesus in their home. Martha is used to portray the busy active Christian, doing lots of good works, but not really a very spiritual person. Mary, on the other hand, is seen as the contemplative Christian, sitting at Jesus' feet, listening to his every word.

The punch line of this interpretation of that passage is Jesus' own words, "Mary has chosen what is good..." The conclusion being that inactive contemplation is better, more spiritual, than doing good works. I am not convinced that Jesus was trying place relative values on two ways of life. The point that he was trying to make was that Mary chose the right thing to do at the right time; that is the important lesson.

Our way of seeing this as two role models for spirituality comes to us through monastic eyes. The plain fact is that in life there are the Marys and the Marthas. The Marthas should not get upset that the Marys aren't 'down to earth,' but neither should the Marys try to make the Marthas feel spiritually inadequate. Both need to value the other and learn the need for discernment as to when to be a Martha and when to be a Mary.

At this point, I want to make it very clear that I am not trying to say that monastic spirituality is wrong, or that I think monks and nuns see themselves as a spiritual elite. I absolutely believe that the vows they take and the service that they render is a God given calling. As I have said above, we need to affirm and support them, something which Protestant churches are not very good at doing.

The spiritual insights that they teach us should not be thrown aside either. The greatness and mystery of God must never be forgotten. Down whichever path you are led in your search for God, the one thing that will take you the farthest is this principle that monastic and mystical writers show: there will always be much more to God than you already know, and there will always be much more to God than you can ever know. Devotion, however you choose to express it, is the key to exploring all the depths and riches of God's love for you.

Hold onto to this in the times when God feels the closest and it will not only save you from spiritual pride, but it will also lead you even further. Hold onto this truth when it feels as if God is remote, and it can become an anchor of hope, reaching into depths that you have not yet seen.

Nonetheless, it is important to recognise that monastic spirituality is just that. It is a prayerful life for people who are living a contemplative lifestyle and as such is the right model for those called to it, but that does not necessarily make it the right model for those who are not called to it.

In the same way, I do want to give the impression that I am saying you should never have a quiet-time or go on a retreat. From time to time, the stress of our society creates a need in us to take time and set it aside solely for God. Even so, we require a different set of ideas about our relationship with God, other than those that are traditionally associated with the quiet-time.

Monastic spirituality is a full time way of life and, in a way, the quiet-time style of personal prayer attempts to reach for this contemplative prayer life, within the bounds of our ordinary human lives, but by its very nature it will always fall short of what it is aiming for. There will never be enough time for us to do all that a contemplative spiritual life requires. In fact, for many people, their commitments to work and relationships make it extremely difficult to even find the personal space to have any effective time of prayer.

I have heard preachers argue that surely everyone can find half an hour here or there for devotion, but the answer I have also heard from many people in the pews is a resounding, "No!" Having two boys of my own, and wanting to play an equal part in their upbringing, I can say quite categorically there were at least four years of nappies, sleepless nights and early mornings when it was physically impossible to have a quiet-time at all without abandoning my family commitments all together.

If the quiet-time is considered to be the only anchor between us and God, then it is not surprising that, during these times in particular, our experience is that God is not The Nearest, but is in fact The Furthest.

I know that I am not alone in this. I have several encounters in my mind with people I have seen juggling their various commitments and finding that the quiet-time to be just one ball too many. I do not for one minute think that we should patronisingly suggest they drop one their other balls. Life is not always that simple.

One encounter, for instance, was with a friend who works in a busy office. Under normal circumstances his workload normally fills every minute of his working day and he goes home quite exhausted. In his 'spare' time he has to study for the exams that his job requires him to take, his wife has had their first baby and his church would like him to lead a Bible study group. To add to these stresses, he confessed the guilt he feels because he either cannot have a quiet-time, or if he does, finds it is governed by all the pressures that come flooding in the moment he sits down. What he really needs is not a good quiet-time, but a good break!

Another encounter was with a different friend whose life is almost the opposite of the office worker. She is single and is suffering the despondency many feel when they have been unemployed for a few years. Finding the motivation to do anything at all has become arduous in the least.

Many mornings there seems to be little point in getting up: there is nothing much to get up for. Some days she finds she is able to read her Bible, and on those days she goes over the top, trying to catch up on a week's unread readings. Other days she feels the possibility of prayer seems a million miles away, because it would mean yet another admission of failure to match up to the devotional ideal that a 'real' Christian should reach.

Yet another person I know, caught up the urban work ethic, gets up at 6.30 am in order to leave home at 7.30 p.m. and return home again eleven or twelve hours later, before finishing the day with a church meeting at 8pm.

Traditionally, we have said to these people, "In addition to all these things, if you seriously love God, you must also find time for your personal devotions" ...and we are back, once again, in the realms of measuring our love for God in terms of the quantity and quality of time we spend alone with him.

Realistically, we have to ask, where can people such as these find the space for a concentrated and effective period of personal devotions? After all, the point about having a quiet-time is not just to go through the actions, but for them to make a real impact on our lives. It would take a brave person to tell to them they ought to get out of bed an hour earlier or stay up an hour later, as if that would solve everything. In any case, I have tried both, and the result was the same. Either way, I usually fell asleep after a few minutes.

This conflict between the demands of life and our spirituality is not solely restricted to those outside of full-time Christian ministry; in talking with other ministers I have found that many share the same struggle. Some use the excuse of spirituality being a part of their work and so have their devotions after the children have gone to school or the partner has gone to work. Which all sounds very well, we wouldn't want ministers who do not pray would we? On the other hand, this does appear to give them an unfair advantage over those in secular jobs. The question needs to be asked whether the collection money which pays their stipends should really be spent upon an activity during work hours which the ministers themselves insist is one which every Christian should do in their private time.

On the other hand, I have talked with other ministers who do manage to keep a routine of daily devotions, but do so at the expense of sharing family responsibilities with their partners.

For all these people, there must be another way, other than the traditional quiet-time which, far from bringing God close, can sometimes distance him even further from the lives they are caught up in. All these people I have talked about are real, they all love God wholeheartedly but feel, as I used to feel, that if the Christian's relationship with God is so strictly dependent on having devotions, then he must be virtually The Furthest from us, not The Nearest.

As I delved into the roots of the quiet-time, its ideology and the question of whether it really is the only model for personal spirituality, I eventually found a ray of hope, and I found it in the model of the Gospel of Christ.

Jesus came into our world to be the presence of God with us in our world and in all that our lives entail. Incarnation - that is the beginning of the Gospel. In the stories of Jesus stilling storms he does not transport the disciples to the safety of the shore; in one account he comes to them from the shore, whilst in the other he is already in the same boat with them, but in neither account does he whisk them away from the storm.

He saves us not by removing us from the world, but by being with us, sharing in all that we experience, and by healing and restoring us where we are. Surely this is what we should take to form the basis for a model of Christian spirituality.

God is no longer remote, up there, The Furthest, but in Jesus he is Emmanuel, God with you, The Nearest. Now he is nearer to you than the storm. He is in the same boat with you. He is infinitely nearer to you even than a quiet-time.

## CHAPTER 3

# THE NEAREST FOR THE ORDINARY

If you ever find yourself feeling motivated to go out and do something after reading an inspiring book, give your brain a chance to count up to ten, very slowly, over the course of a few days...

At an early stage in my Christian life I found myself reading the biography of a man called Smith Wigglesworth. Here was an uneducated plumber who was so touched by God that whenever he entered the pulpit he spoke with the most beautiful clarity. It was said that he exuded the presence of God so powerfully that people would often fall to their knees begging to be saved without him having to say a word.

It was one of those books that read like a missing chapter from the Book of Acts. It helped you to see some of the possibilities of a life totally and unreservedly dedicated to seeking and following the will of God. At the time I found the book very inspiring and a challenge to my own pitiful efforts at evangelism. I rushed through it in a matter of days, wearing appropriate blinkers which skilfully obscured the bits that talked of the cost of living such a life, but devouring the anecdotes of the miracles and the healings.

When I finished the book, I was filled with that same sort of excitement that I used to get as teenager who, having been to watch a kung-fu or spy film, would be inspired to go out of the cinema and bruise the side of my hand on the trunk of the nearest tree. Unfortunately I confused that excitement with the motivation of the Holy Spirit and immediately felt that I had to go out and try this fantastic spiritual power myself. I had no doubts that God could not do these things. It was perfectly obvious to me that all I had to do was copy Smith Wigglesworth's example, tell just one or two people about Jesus, and the result would be an instant revival in the town.

I suppose my thought process went like this: Smith was a normal, average person, I was a normal, average person; he was a person who loved God and believed in the power of the Holy Spirit, I was a person who loved God and believed in the power of the Holy Spirit; whenever he spoke about Gospel people were saved, therefore if I spoke about the Gospel, people would also fall on their knees in repentance, mass revival would follow and I would become an internationally famous preacher.

I grabbed hold of Lindsay, a friend with whom I was living at the time, (who incidentally, really does have a gift for evangelism) and managed to persuade him that the moment to go witnessing was at hand, and that if we didn't go out in the driving February rain, countless souls could be lost.

Strangely, the town was almost deserted in the needle-like, near horizontal precipitation, and there was no waiting multitude in sight. Undaunted we made our way to the railway station. I think I must have had that I'm-going-to-give-you-this-leaflet-whether-you-like-it-or-not look on my face because the few passengers who were waiting for buses or taxis, saw us coming and disappeared into town as if we were Jehovah's Witnesses trying to sell double glazing.

One man remained. He was dressed in clothes that he obviously wore twenty-four hours a day and was slumped in the shelter of a wall that was probably also his home. I made sure I didn't let myself see these details, but boosted myself up with a more soul-converting thought, "This must be the one meant for the Kingdom!" I concluded, "His reason for staying behind is clearly a hunger for The Truth ". Actually the real reason that he had not managed to escape was contained in the bottle concealed in the brown paper bag he was clutching; and the vaguely hopeful look on his face came from a different sort of hunger.

Before Lindsay could stop me, I had leaped upon my prey and had managed to extract a confession for Christ that even the Inquisition would have been proud of. It wasn't exactly my fault that the only words the tramp was able to mutter in response to my interrogation were, "Yersh" and "Urrp". Then, doing my best to carry the air of the faithful servant in victory, I followed Lindsay home. Secretly, I was somewhat dejected and felt a little less like Smith Wigglesworth but a little more like Tim Ross.

We all like to read those stories of great spiritual giants who have set the world aflame with their zeal for God. It is inspiring to hear about those who have shown incredible confidence and assurance in tragedy which has brought them through to triumph; or those whose faith has accomplished some wonderful task against all human odds.

Oswald Chambers (author of the devotional commentary, My Utmost For The Highest) had a reputation for getting up at the crack of dawn and praying until he felt that God was truly present with him, however long that would take. John Wesley whittled his sleep down to an absolute minimum so that he could not only pray and read his Bible before breakfast, but also study classical, spiritual writings in their original languages. Martin Luther was born to a peasant family but ended up changing the course of Church history.

Even so, stories of people like these are double edged, with encouragement cutting one way and a feeling that is something like spiritual impotence cutting the other. We are encouraged because we begin to see that what we believe actually works, and that what we are aiming for must be humanly achievable. But (and it is a big 'but') how often have you read their biographies and said to yourself, "That is fine for them, but I am not like that. I do not have the same kind of temperament or circumstances or faith as they did." Their examples are wonderful, we have to admit, yet we find ourselves also admitting that we would be grateful if only we could achieve one tenth of what they achieved.

As I say, we need inspiring stories to encourage and motivate us, but how often are those people held up before us by well-meaning preachers not just as unique individuals, but also as a standard for measuring Christians who are truly committed to God? "This is what happens," those preachers say, "when you are truly committed to God." The inference being that if we are not achieving great things (from a human perspective), or if our lives are spent mostly in normal secular pursuits, then we are not wholly dedicated to God as Chambers, Luther, and Wesley were.

This false logic can sometimes go a step further to forge a link between the achievements of these spiritual giants and their devotional life. They accomplished their deeds, the argument goes, because they were great men and women of prayer, meaning they spent a lot of time in devotions. This leaves us feeling that we will only really get to know God, have a sense of his presence and be an effective Christian (whatever that means) when we have perfected a devotional discipline that follows a similar pattern to theirs.

Perhaps you can begin to see how such thinking might hold back your developing relationship with God. If knowing God is so precariously perched on the success of your achieving the right level of private devotions, then you could easily be tempted to put up with a second-class relationship in favour of a way of life that seems beyond the capabilities of the average person, or is outside of the restrictions that your life imposes upon you.

Your relationship with God becomes second-class when it is easier to give the nod to actions and deeds associated with commitment than it is to take on all that appears to be required for an intimate relationship with him. "If that is what God requires for true commitment," you say to yourself, "then God will just have to put up with me not being very committed." You resign yourself to live your life assuming that God will have to accept that a truly close relationship with him is beyond your reach, and that, as a result, he will remain distant from you when in fact he really is not.

Surely God cannot have so made us in such a way that it is the most difficult thing of all for us to know him? The answer is quite simply, "No." We are made in the image of God, the Bible says, and the whole panorama of God's dealings with the human race in the Bible shows us that he wants us to know him. That is the purpose of our existence. He would be a perverse God indeed if he created us in such a way that it was all but impossible to fulfil the purpose for which he made us.

The next time you walk through a busy high street or market place, look at the enormous variety of individuals there and remind yourself of this: God wants to be near to them, to be known to them and by them, every one. And he made them for that purpose. God is the Nearest for the Ordinary, not just super spiritual giants, not just those who are free to spend countless hours in prayer and contemplation.

At times though, it can appear as if the opposite is true and you identify more with Paul's struggles. The very thing that you want to do, to love God, heart and soul, is impossible, whilst you find yourself unable to resist doing the very things that deny your love for God. You should not think that this is caused by any lack of faith or love for God on your part. Paul, who had the same experience, could hardly be said to be lacking in faith! These conflicts are a part of your continuing struggle in developing a life that is centred on God rather than on self or, as Paul expresses it, putting off the old self and putting on the new.

...which can be another source of problems, and is how some Christians have quite literally made a rod for their own backs.

Jesus does indeed call us to deny ourselves, to take up our cross and follow him. That call is something we need to take very seriously. At the same time, a growing intimacy with God is a blessing of the Christian life, but we should be cautious about claiming that the latter is a consequence of the former. (It all depends upon how you understand the phrase "take up your cross", something we will look at later.) We should be even more wary about asserting that an awareness of God's love can only come with the deepest kind of commitment shown in the lives of notable Christian men and women.

Once you associate the knowledge and nearness of God with increasing levels of commitment, then another problem emerges. If you succeed in getting to a stage where you are conscious of God's presence, or find a sense of peaceful assurance, you might then be tempted to assume that you must have reached a greater level of sanctification and spiritual commitment. The most elementary understanding of grace tells you that you can never assume that. Even though you should always urge yourself on to a deeper and greater level of self-denial to God's will, you must never allow yourself think of self-denial as a means to gain anything from God. Self-denial is about changing your orientation to God, not his orientation to you.

Any approach to prayer and devotions which contains the elements of doing spiritual activity in order to gain God's blessings and presence risks turning God into a kind of cosmic vending machine. If we put the right coinage in, out will come the desired product. We are effectively paying God to bless us. In this instance, the coinage is the commitment, faith and depths of prayer that we feel we ought to be capable of, and the chocolate bar represents answers to prayer and a deeper knowledge of and closeness to God.

No model of prayer which develops these kinds of ideas is helpful, because it is not based on God's grace, our gratitude, or mutual love. It is, at best, a bargain struck with a God who is regarded as holding back his blessing until the right dues have been paid. More importantly, these contractual associations cast a veil over God, putting him back in the inner sanctuary of the temple, waiting to be fed the appropriate sacrifices, whereas he is longing to be the Nearest to all, even the very poorest in terms of spiritual currency.

One of the most liberating yet seemingly contradictory principles of Christian spirituality is that an awareness of your spiritual poverty and dependence on God is absolutely essential for devotion and spiritual growth. For one thing, it is the truest form of confession, based on the total honesty of laying yourself completely open to God, and for another, it makes you all the more conscious of your own need of God as the only spiritual resource in your walk with him. The one thing it must never be confused with, though, is self-deprecation and self-condemnation, which is simply flagellation in another form.

*****

There are those who find self-discipline and living an ordered, methodical life relatively easy. They are the kind of people who find comfort in or even revel in routine, habit and order. For these people, sticking to regular daily devotions is not something they will find difficult or demanding, quite the reverse, in fact. I confess that I envy them a little, because the basic struggles that many of us have to deal with pose no obstacle at all to their spirituality. For them, many of the questions that I am raising in this book may well be meaningless.

I am not ordered. I need to ring the changes to free my creativity. Regular routine in anything is something I find stifling and, perhaps as a consequence, I do struggle with self-discipline. I let God down and disappoint myself because I balk at self-sacrifice and make as many excuses as I can to cut the cost. In a way, I am the most selfish person that I know. On the other hand, I love God, and I do not kid myself that he does not see and understand my many flaws.

I say this to illustrate the Catch-22 of the Christian life, which is that you must have this awareness of your own need of God so that you can grow closer to him. But this comes with a warning, once you have this awareness of your weaknesses, it will actually grow rather than lessen the more you know God. Sometimes it will appear as if the closer you get to God, the less perfect you become.

This, though, is only the appearance of things. In reality, it is an example of the illustration sometimes given by preachers of a hand brought close to a light. Away from the light the hand appears relatively clean, but as the hand is approaches the light more and more dirt appears on it. The hand is not actually getting any dirtier, it is simply that the light is illuminating the dirt more clearly the closer it gets.

The fact of the matter is that world-changing Christians and spiritual giants are special people, gifted by the Holy Spirit. That is why they are chosen for the work they do. Commitment is undoubtedly a factor in works of the Spirit, but what these people accomplish they do primarily through God's grace, which calls them, equips them and works through them and their openness and willingness to respond to the call.

The argument I've been making works the other way too. You should not assume for one minute that all you have to do is get your spirituality and good works up to standard, and a similar calling will follow, or that the dreams and visions will appear as if you have suddenly tuned in to the right God channel. Likewise, you should not continually criticise yourself that your spiritual life is not "up to standard", because you have not yet heard a calling to convert a multitude or turn water into wine. What God does through you, he does because he chooses you, and this choice is not based on your having gained enough merit, or fitted yourself out with exactly the right spiritual clothing, it is based solely on his grace and love for you.

One of the consequences of the charismatic renewal, with its particular emphasis on discovering and using the particular gifts that God has given to each of us, is that it can appear, when taken to the extreme, as if every Christian is specifically called to a world-changing ministry like Billy Graham or St Francis. When our lives fail to produce such a ministry, we feel there must be some significant, underlying reason, but why is it that the first place we look for an answer is the mirror?

Perhaps the real desire that underlies many a quest for ministry, is the desire to feel that one's life is of worth and has meaning. No one wants to feel that their life will pass without having made a mark in some way; we all want to be special and unique.

And so you are. What is more, it is your uniqueness that God loves and values the most. Far more than any type of service or ministry you may be able to offer him. You mean more to God than the sum of all your actions, spiritual or otherwise. Find God and let yourself be found by him, and let that fulfil your desire for meaning and worth.

The causes of this success-oriented approach to spirituality are not all religious. I saw someone interviewed on television who described herself as a "Vertical Transportation Attendant." She worked in the futuristic tower in Seattle called the Space Needle... as a lift operator!

Western society in particular has become more fragmented, with people finding that the only way their existence can be recognised is if they have made a mark on it somehow. Window cleaners are called "vision clearance executives," office cleaners are called "Environment Improvement Technicians" and a "Dispatch Services Facilitator" is someone who works in the post room; all renamed to give their positions an air of importance.

This ethos has filtered into the life of the Church too, with a tangible pressure to be somebody, to have a ministry or face being a second class Christian.

It is not hard to see secular parallels between some of the great Christian leaders and preachers, and the world of politics, commerce and industry. There are many who have made their mark as stateswomen and men or business tycoons who achieved their work with similar sacrifice and single-minded devotion; by existing on three hours of sleep every night and having two-business meetings before a working breakfast. Yet we would not really want to hold up success-oriented worka-holism at the expense of personal relationships as the ideal model of working life. Why then do we do so with spirituality?

It is as if we have translated this ethic into the language and values of Christianity so that the message reads, "Committed Christians are successful Christians, and successful Christians are the ones making a mark in the church." If this is so, then we have no choice but to conclude that if we are not making our mark, we are not successful and must, therefore, be lacking in true commitment.

It's this word 'commitment' which is so misleading. Whenever we hear commitment mentioned, we instantly associate it with time and actions. If we see someone spending every living moment on their work, we say they are committed to it. If a particular project or task is going to require a lot of time and energy to achieve it, we say that it will take commitment.

...which is how you end up judging your worth to God in terms of how you function as a Christian or what you do in the church.

In fact, commitment is not chiefly about the amount of time you spend on a particular task, it is primarily about the way in which you approach it. Commitment is about attitude, rather than actions. It's about where the focus of your heart and will lie. After all, it is perfectly possible to spend every waking moment on an undertaking but have no real commitment to it – that's not commitment though, it's duty.

Real success, in Christian terms, begins when you start to accept your worth to God for who you are, not what you do. This completely changes the way we understand the nature of commitment, which then becomes about wholeheartedly offering who you are to him as your devotion. What you do for God, what we call ministry, doesn't come into the equation at all.

Then, armed with a truthful awareness of your place in the love of God, and an honest openness of your life before him, whatever you choose to do, whether it is in the life of the church, in secular work or in your leisure time, becomes both devotion and ministry.

What we have come to is this: The value God places on us is not, as ours so often is, based on the level and number of Christian duties we perform for him. Nor is it founded on how good we are, morally speaking. The meaning of success, in God's kingdom, Jesus tells us, is seen in a child, who he places in the centre of our adult world. What matters to Jesus can be seen in a woman caught in adultery, who he sends away, unharmed by religious, moral and social judgement. Devotion, Jesus shows us, can be found in the actions of a woman lavishing expensive perfume upon his feet. Where others could only see the practical value of her gift and how it might be better used, Jesus' gaze was firmly fixed upon her and the value of her love for him.

The most incredible, miraculous thing is that Jesus chooses to expresses his ministry, in the main, through so-called ordinary Christians. It is a crucial principal of the New Testament that Jesus' ministry is now carried out through the whole Body of Christ, not just one or two 'special' followers. That is the way of Kingdom; he does indeed choose the weak things of the world to shame the wise, but he does not always transform them into the strong and brilliantly clever after he has chosen them. No, he chooses me, and he chooses you.

The Church is not made up entirely of spiritual giants, nor is it meant to be. For the most part, we are just normal Christians, going about our lives, trying to serve God as he wants us to. Without putting any question on our love for the Lord, it is a simple fact that most of us are not able to pray and study for two or three hours before breakfast; most of us will not spend our lives converting thousands of people at rallies around the globe; most of us cannot cut ourselves off from the world and spend our entire time in devotional worship and Bible study, but God is still The Nearest for us. More specifically, he is no less The Nearest for us than he is for those who are able (or are called to) all those things.

God is The Nearest for the Ordinary. This is the Gospel we see so clearly reflected in the life of Jesus. He is not just The Nearest for James, Peter and John; he is not just The Nearest to St Ignatius, Mother Teresa and Billy Graham. He is The Nearest; God with us, as much as and no less than he is with those whom we regard as the spiritual masters or the religious professionals.

Jesus was just as near to the other disciples whose only mention is a name in a list. He was the Nearest for a widow, a woman at a well, a prostitute, a soldier, a beggar and all those others who don't have names and yet who followed Jesus with the disciples. God was near to all the hundreds of thousands of devoted Christians throughout the last two thousand years, people whose names never made into a history book or biography, yet who served their Lord faithfully and loved him deeply, just as those whose names did. So he is near to us.

The Gospels show us something else too. They show us a God who reaches out to touch the lepers, who steps aside to meet the beggars and who lifts up the lame. In other words they show us that God's nature is to go out of his way to meet the weak. What we do not see is a God who holds himself up as a golden reward for only the supremely spiritual fit. Why, then, do we persist in regarding spirituality as some kind of a marathon where only those who have the stamina for hours of prayerful solitude can win the prize? Indeed, why do we hold onto any notions that the presence of God is prize which can only be won with hard graft and super spiritual fitness?

What the Gospel says is, "In Jesus, God has come to me." It is a message of which we must continually remind ourselves. If you did nothing else but say that to yourself every day, it could transform your relationship with God.

At those times when any form of spiritual activity is beyond our ability, it is a message of deep assurance. At other times, when we feel fully in control and self-disciplined, it is a humble reminder that it is grace upon which we depend for an encounter with God, not our own efforts.

He is the Nearest for you now, at this moment and at this stage of your Christian life. He is here to meet you now where you are, in whatever "here" you find yourself. He is not waiting at some point of spiritual maturity further down the road on your Christian pilgrimage, in the hope that you may eventually arrive there to meet him. He is with you now, and is closer even than your next step.

This does not mean that there is no challenge left, or that spirituality now requires no effort or commitment on your part. Nor does it mean that Jesus, having come to meet you, does not then call you on, to take that next faltering step. Jesus still says, "If any of you wants to be my follower, you must turn from your selfish ways, take up your cross daily, and follow me" (Luke 9:23 New Living Translation).

The invalid at the pool at Bethesda had been there thirty-eight years. With no prospect of employment and no source of income, his "here" was lying beside the pool all day, every day in the hope of a cure from the waters. For thirty-eight years he failed to get into the water at the right time. We can't guess his motives, but probably the only thing that kept him at the pool was the simple fact that he had nowhere else to go, nothing else to do and no other source of hope.

Jesus came to him there, at the pool. He met with him in his "here" and talked with him, but it wasn't just a comfort visit from a local celebrity. Jesus also challenged him to take up his bed and walk.

Whilst Jesus is not waiting for you to take that next step before he will meet you, he does challenge you to grow and move on in your pilgrimage with him and to continue to explore the love and grace of God with him.

So what does all this mean then? If God is not just The Nearest for those in the spiritual super-league (the Body of Christ metaphor in 1 Corinthians Chapter 12 is fairly clear that there is no super-league), but he is also The Nearest for the Ordinary, how does this affect the way we think about prayer and devotion? Fundamentally, it means is that there must be a way for the Ordinary to seek and find him that does not make us feel we need to have 'arrived' at the perfect devotional life first.

He would not be a just God if he gave himself only to the spiritual elite, or if he reserved the greater part of his love, blessing and presence for those whose discipleship and devotions were practically perfect. It would also go against the principle of God's grace over our own efforts.

Perfect discipleship is not the starting point of walking with Jesus; nor do you have to be able to have the perfect quiet-time to find him and walk with him. The challenge of a life lived closely aware of the presence of God is not to increase the frequency or intensity of devotional acts, but to aim for a completeness in our desire for God and a love for him that is wholehearted. Then the goal shifts from aiming to achieve a perfect life (perfect spiritual and practical deeds), to aiming to achieve a perfect love.

*****

Brother Lawrence, a French Lay Brother serving in a Carmelite

Monastery in the seventeenth Century, discovered the secret of living always in the presence of God. He called it, "The Practice of the Presence." As a lay brother, he worked in the kitchens and as a cobbler, doing the kind of day-to-day tasks which may have otherwise kept the monks from their prayers and studies. Though he loved God very deeply this meant that he was not able to spend long periods in prayer, as the monks did. Instead he found that, by keeping his love for God awake in his consciousness all the time he was doing his daily duties, he was able to live continually in the presence of God.

"It is only necessary," he says, "to realise that God is intimately present with us, to turn every moment to him and ask for his help" (The Practice of the Presence, Brother Lawrence, translated by E.M. Blaiklock, © 1981, Hodder & Stoughton, p28).

Lay brothers, like Brother Lawrence, were under limited vows and had to take occasional retreats and periods of withdrawal. The reason for this was that their menial tasks were seen to be a distraction from prayerful living and so it was thought that they needed these quiet days to focus their lives once more on God and regain a sense of his presence.

Brother Lawrence, however, found these retreats to be an unnecessary burden. "He neither wanted them, nor asked for them, because his most demanding task did not divert him from God" (Ibid. p24). In fact he calls the belief that times of prayer are essentially different to other times, a deception.

Whether you are deep in prayer or totally absorbed in your work, enjoying your hobby or sharing a meal or a coffee with a friend, God is no further away, and yet, how often do you measure his closeness by the amount of prayer you have done or the degree of prayer you are capable of?

What Brother Lawrence shows us is how easy it is to lock God away in the prayer closet and monastic cell, and to make knowing his presence in our lives something that we only associate with strict devotional practices or special circumstances. In turn, this makes us feel that the presence of God is accessible only to those Christians with the time and inclination to create the special circumstances that deep and intense prayer requires.

It is no wonder that many non-believers are convinced that Christians are out of touch with the reality of daily life, and that prayer is a sort of head-in-the-clouds business. Yet you cannot see God more present in real life, or more in touch with ordinary people, than in the life of Jesus.

He is the Nearest for the Ordinary.

# CHAPTER 4

# DEVOTED TO THE NEAREST

I had gone with a friend to her church for the weekly Bible study. Along with the rest of the congregation, I was sitting with my Bible, a notepad and the obligatory highlighter pens, which were all the rage in those days. The minister announced the theme for the night, "What To Do In Your Quiet-time" and in front of us, on the overhead projector screen, was a pie-chart. It was a very beautiful, neat pie chart, divided into equally neat coloured segments, each one with a different title; Praise, Thanksgiving, Silence, Bible reading, Confession, Personal Prayer and Intercession.

"These are the elements that need to be included in a quiet-time," he explained, "and it really doesn't matter if each section is only short."

This was a very comforting start. The intercessory part of my devotions was frequently a one line after-thought usually beginning with the words, "Oh, and please help..."

The minister then went on to explain the time element involved: "Yes, with careful thought and planning, these can easily be fitted into a one hour quiet-time."

"ONE HOUR!" I thought, "God's lucky if he gets fifteen minutes of bleary-eyed mumblings between getting out of bed and eating toast." Daily devotions in my early days as a Christian varied in length quite a bit; I think I did manage the full hour once. More usually they were short and consisted mostly of apologies for the poverty of my prayers.

In fact, at that point in time, I could easily have replaced the minister's complicated pie chart with a much simpler one. The first segment in my devotional pie began with an act of confession. Something along the lines of, "Lord, I'm sorry I haven't prayed much in the last few days." Then I would progress to the next segment... further confession. "I really am sorry I haven't had a proper quiet-time this week." This section formed the core of my quiet-time, so occasionally I would indulge myself and extend it for longer than usual, but I always like to finish with a note of thanksgiving; "Thank you Lord, that the Bible says, 'If we confess our sins, you are faithful and just and will forgive us'... sorry I don't pray more... Amen."

Imagine my delight when I found on the shelves of a Christian bookshop a little booklet with the appealing title, "The Ten Minute Devotional". Here was a goal I stood a chance of reaching. With enough determination, I felt I really might be able to build up to ten minutes with God almost every day.

Incredibly, a few weeks later I came across another book of daily prayers that matched my prayer attention span even more closely, it was simply called, "Five minutes with God."

This set me thinking; perhaps I might be able to come up with the ultimate guide in devotional brevity for those who shared my devotional struggles. I'd call it, "Just a Second Lord."

Not very long after becoming a Christian I learned that I was supposed to have a purposeful quiet-time every day in order to maintain a healthy relationship with God. Once I'd made the connection between those two things, the next few years of my Christian life were largely governed by a sense of guilt and failure. I found it difficult to pray regularly and in addition had not the self-discipline to get up early enough to have an hour's prayer and Bible reading. I experimented with different times of day, but to no avail.

In the mornings when I did manage to crack the dawn, devotions were a dead loss. My brain could not get into gear and I could easily be distracted by the fascination of a paper clip, which could be bent into odd shapes during meaningful silences. Evenings were just as bad. I was tired, concentrating was difficult, so I would rattle off the prayers as briefly as possible and get on with reading a good book (but not always The Good Book).

I even tried praying whilst going for an early morning walk. This last attempt worked the best, as the process of walking prevented me from going back to sleep. I still had difficulty concentrating that early in the day, but at least the exercise was very beneficial.

I tried another tack. It occurred to me that if I had the right engaging devotional aids, I could develop a good habit. My first attempt to get my devotions sorted out was to try a simple Through-The-Bible-In-A-Year reading plan. I began in June and faithfully completed that month's quota of scripture passages. When September arrived, I thought I might, perhaps, switch to a three-year Bible plan instead. My new habit-of-a-lifetime broke down somewhere in mid August, because the required daily chunks of Bible were so huge. Needless to say, the three-year plan proved just as unsuccessful as the one-year plan.

It wasn't so much that I wasn't getting anywhere with the readings. It was more that when I did do them, I got bogged down on bits that I wanted to explore more deeply and consequently took them too far. This in turn meant that I would get behind with the readings, or that I was put off from doing them because I felt I didn't have the time to absorb them fully. I was reading the Bible because it was there.

In the end I decided to go for something less ambitious than the whole Bible so I turned to that section of devotional commentaries whose titles all begin, "Through the year with..." or "Daily Thoughts By..."

Once again I fell into the trap of catch-up guilt. The trouble was that I would miss a few days and the next prayer time became a bit like homework sessions where I tried to catch up. I am not sure what you call somebody who collects prayer manuals, but, apart from the monthly booklets one can buy, I now have six devotional books, all unfinished.

The heart of my problem, I knew, was one of self-discipline. I am not a person who is happy in routines. I am not one of those people who have no problems with keeping to patterns and habits, just the opposite, in fact.

Which raises another relatively serious question about patterns and habits of prayer. Just as there is an implied relationship between the frequency of prayer time and the presence of God, it is easy to make a connection between spirituality and discipline, which again risks exchanging the grace of God for spirituality by merit.

This is not too surprising when you consider the strongly disciplined background that individual spirituality has had. From the strict asceticism of the desert fathers to the regulated lives of medieval monks, the emphasis has been on a devotion to discipline as an expression of devotion to God. The more disciplined a person was in their life, the more devout they were perceived to be. Conversely, the less ordered someone was in their devotions, the less spiritual they must be (how often have you used that argument with yourself?).

One immediate consequence of this unfortunate association between devotion to God and the ability to lead an organized spiritual life is that it can foster a sense of guilt and give false goals to those who cannot easily achieve this. You feel guilty or unspiritual because a regular and meaningful quiet-time eludes you and the only conceivable appeasement to this guilt is to spend the rest of your life striving "to be more disciplined."

Quite subtly, the goal in your devotions shifts towards being able to meet some hazy ideal of a disciplined life instead of a closer relationship with God. You have linked spiritual contentment with the practice of prayer rather than with its object.

On the other hand, we are all too aware that that the word

"disciple" is closely related to the word "discipline". As I will show in the last chapter, I do not want to give the impression that I think that there is no need for discipline in the Christian's life. What I am saying is that we need to be careful to avoid associating a person's ability to perform the acts we associate with a meaningful devotional pattern with the reward of closeness with God.

Teaching about the practice of personal spirituality sometimes fails to take into account that many people struggle with exactly the kind of problems I have been talking about. From the perspective of the gospels, spirituality begins where we are. Jesus comes to us on our begging mat by the pool, and begins a relationship with us here.

The plain fact is that self-discipline comes much easier to some than to others, and it should not be assumed that this is due to their being weak-willed or lazy. In which case, God cannot have purposed that only those capable of routine and habit should find a close relationship with him whilst those of us who find self-discipline more difficult are deprived of it.

Traditionally, spirituality as it is interpreted in our get-ahead stay-ahead world actually favours those who find self-discipline easy or who thrive on a habitual and methodical approach to life. There really are people who wake up alert every morning at 5.30am, who then slot in a neat one-hour pie-chart spiritual breakfast before their toast and marmalade. All the same, it takes a brave (or blinkered) person to say that we should all be like that.

If, as you read this you find yourself saying, "If I can manage it anyone can." consider those for whom making a new habit is just as difficult as it is for someone else to break a lifelong one.

Having said all that, what are the options: get organized or feel guilty? Certainly, that was the circular trap in which I was caught for a fairly lengthy phase at the beginning of my Christian life.

There was no light bulb of revelation that ended this period. It was more a slow turning up of the dimmer switch. Gradually I realized that I had been praying so hard about how I wasn't praying that I had actually spent more time in prayer than if I had had a short quiet-time and left it at that.

"Dimmer" more properly describes my mental processes at this stage, because it took another few years before I thought to ask myself when and, more specifically, why I did all this praying about my devotions.

The answer to the "when" I saw, was not first thing in the morning or last thing at night, but nearly all the time. I had muttered my apologetic prayers to God in all the spare moments between tasks, on the way to shops, going to appointments and at other similar times. These had been the times when I had talked to God.

The "why" behind this concerned praying came as something of a revelation, which should have been obvious to me from the start (I blame the dimmer switch). The reason I was saying all these prayers about my lack of 'proper' prayer, I realized, was because my heart was devoted to God and yearned for a closer walk with him. As a matter of fact, this was often the subject of those moments of prayer.

They were not times of deep spiritual awareness or great intercession, but they were still genuine moments of prayer. As the dimmer switch was turned up, I began to see that if I could only turn those moments of self-pitying prayer into real but brief moments of devotion focussed on God, I wouldn't have just the obligatory half hour daily devotional; my whole day would be filled with prayer. Once I had taken that a few tentative steps in that directions, I was hit with a thought that came as a flash of illumination:

What God wants from us is devotion not devotions.

What he longs for is a devoted life not just a life of devotions, and I knew that I loved him.

It was a verse in Hosea that spun the dimmer suddenly around to full, "For I desire mercy, not sacrifice, and an acknowledgment of God rather than burnt offerings" (6:6). I had read that verse many times before, but without particular significance. Reading it this time, from the perspective of my explorations into prayer, I began to see that I had been concentrating so much on trying to get the means of prayer right, that I had lost sight of the object of prayer. It was as though I had a dietary problem and was trying to sort it out by simply changing the cutlery.

I am sure Biblical commentators will cringe at this, but in the context of my thoughts and struggle with prayer, "I desire mercy, not sacrifice" I read as "I desire devotion not devotions" and devotion was something I knew I had within me. What I then set my mind to was how to develop devotion to God as a moment-by-moment relationship instead of shoe-horning it into a daily God-slot.

***** 

The underlying problem with spending your life trying to achieve the model quiet-time is that it is easy to fall into the trap of "doing your devotions" because they have got to be done. Devotions themselves can never be a substitute for a relationship with God.

A part of this problem is terminology. We often talk about our spirituality as our "Prayer Life." There are books that will tell you what to do in your prayer life. Preachers will emphasize the importance of having a stable prayer life. And Christians will compare what they do in their respective prayer lives. All of which can give the impression that our 'prayer life' is some parallel reality, separated off from our ordinary life.

It is as though Christians are expected to lead a double life, like some kind of cartoon super-hero. Most of the time we are ordinary mild-mannered people, going about our everyday lives with little to give away our true identity, but at 6 a.m. the disguise is thrown on and we enter our other life to become (fanfare!) The Praying Christian. I realise it's a far-fetched illustration, but, taken to the extreme, this classification of spirituality as a 'prayer life' puts us in danger of disconnecting devotion to God from the rest of daily life.

This particular problem arises as we try to describe, in graspable terms, what some other religions already recognise, which is that there _is_ a spiritual dimension to life. By its very nature, this dimension is different to the world our senses deal with, but already we are faced with a problem.

By describing it as another dimension or sphere of life the natural conclusion we are drawn to make is that prayer and spirituality must involve some kind of movement in order to enter this dimension. Prayer then becomes a mode that we _go_ into, a concept that I will deal with more fully in a later chapter.

The idea of the Christian life as a journey, as a pilgrimage, is a very old but very helpful one. We do (or should) grow, change and develop in our life with God. We can look back over the years and see how far we have come since our journey with God began.

That is precisely the point; it is both a journey with God and into God. Yet what sometimes happens is that we go a stage further and describe prayer itself as a movement towards God. Although it is sometimes helpful to see prayer in this way, it can actually be a hindrance in our desire to be close to God.

The journey of prayer has been variously described as upward, outward and inward, but always the implication is that it is towards God; that prayer is the vehicle to convey us from where we are to where he is. We can get a clearer picture of this model of prayer if we take a moment to go back over some of the things mentioned in chapter 2 about the monastic roots of the quiet-time.

St Augustine, for instance, a North African bishop at the end of the fourth century, was greatly influenced by the ideas of Plato. As a philosopher, Plato was famous for his metaphor which pictures humanity as living in a dark cave. In this cave humans sit and gaze at the shadows cast on the wall by the light of a fire and, seeing them, suppose them to be reality. Our task in life, as Plato sees it, is to turn from the illusory shadows and make a journey towards the true light of the sun (a metaphor for truth), because only in the light of truth and goodness may we see the true forms of reality – the things themselves, rather than their shadows.

Augustine saw how naturally God filled the role of Truth, Light and Reality in this metaphor. Looked at from this perspective the Christian life becomes a journey out of a godless and fallen world to the true and ultimate reality of God. The purpose of prayer, from Augustine's point of view, is to aid us on this journey towards God. This, he said, is best achieved through the purification of self from worldly desires and by withdrawal from the world through contemplation.

In this it is easy to see the fundamental principles of monastic thought. It is also important to recognise that underlying these principles is a belief that the world is essentially a-theist - without God - and ultimately opposed to his purposes.

There were even Christians in Augustine's time who saw "The World" not just as a metaphor for evil but also as the actual realm of evil in a way which virtually denied God had ever had anything to do with it.

Later founders of monasticism continued to use images of movement in their teaching about prayer. Benedict of Nursia (end of the fifth century AD) used the illustration of a ladder of humility on which we rise to God like the angels ascending on Jacob's Ladder.

In the sixth century Gregory the Great used the metaphor of pilgrimage, though his way of using this illustration sees us in exile, thus our journey is back to the Promised Land and the presence of God. Therefore the purpose of the spiritual life, from Gregory's point of view, is once again to take us from this world to God.

The idea of prayer as both the journey and the vehicle that carries us on that journey continued to be used by Christian mystics. They found this idea of leaving the world behind for the presence of God helpful. Catherine of Sienna (fourteenth century) used the metaphor of the Christian life as a journey on road over a bridge, forged by Christ, between God and us. This journey involves taking three main steps; forsaking the world, denying sin and being filled with love for God.

Teresa of Avila (sixteenth century) talked of prayer as an inward journey to the "Interior Castle". In her very rich allegory, we enter through the door of prayer to escape the sinful world, and journey through the inner courts of the castle to the sanctuary of God's presence.

As I said earlier, what all these writers were trying to do was illustrate their very real and deep devotion for God in terms that others could relate to. They achieved a level of closeness with God that few have managed, but we need to recognize the legacy of their illustrations in the way we regard our relationship with God.

What the mystics' and early Church writers' metaphors do is reinforce the idea of God as distant from our life, which in turn colours our whole understanding of the purpose and nature of prayer.

It might be helpful to think of the ways you can approach prayer as two parallel railway lines, one of which understands prayer as progression towards God, who is regarded as transcendent (above and beyond our universe), thus it travels *to* God, whilst the other line sees prayer as a relationship with God who is immanent (with us in every sphere of life), so it travels *with* God.

Bridges, ladders and journeys from exile are not the only metaphors used for prayer, there are other images taken from the Bible that also revolve around ideas of movement. One example is the account of Jesus' transformation on the Mount of Transfiguration, where the journey of the disciples up the mountain becomes a parallel for the journey into prayer.

In this allegory, the world with all its distractions and problems is left below and it is up on the mountaintop, in the heights (or depths) of prayer, where we begin to encounter Jesus as he really is. The mountaintop experience of seeing Jesus and hearing the voice of God becomes the goal of prayer.

Consequently, if we can pray for long enough or deeply enough (i.e. if we have the right quiet-time), we may be blessed to have this kind of true encounter with God. In fact the goal for many of those contemplative and mystic Christians was to find and maintain the mountaintop experience.

There are still some helpful lessons to be gained here; after all there really are times when prayer is like a mountain to be climbed. Sometimes the presence of God may only be heartbeat away, but there are also times when it is a major effort just to begin the ascent; when every step in prayer requires supreme effort and the presence of God is shrouded with cloud. There are also times when we simply haven't the spiritual energy left to get there at all and it feels as if we are stuck at base camp - which is when mountaintop prayer fails to meet our need.

We know, of course, that there comes a time when we have to come down from the mountain and go back into the real world of ordinary life again. At this point we are often offered another model from the Bible to help us: the model of Moses coming down from Mount Sinai, with his face veiled to cover the after-glow of being in the presence of God. We may not always be able to stay on the mountaintop, it is argued, but if we are devoted enough, we may leave the mount as Moses did, with the glow of God on our faces.

When I was at a Bible College, my digs were about a mile away, this meant a twenty-minute walk into college every day. I can remember quite clearly, when I did manage to have an hour's quiet-time, walking along the road trying squeeze out the Moses glow, in the hope that passers-by might fall to their knees in awe of glory of God flowing from me.

What we sometimes forget is that the vision of the transfiguration was meant to show the disciples their blindness to the Jesus they had already encountered. It was through his walking, talking and teaching in their daily lives that they had already encountered the real Jesus, they just had not realized it. Jesus would go on to tell them that in seeing him they had seen God. Their daily encounter with Jesus was meant to be as much an encounter with God as were the moments of special revelation. In a way, the transfiguration is less of a model for prayer and more of a rebuke for failing to see the real Jesus in our daily lives.

A better model for prayer is that of the disciples called in their work place to walk the highways of life with Jesus. The disciples journey with Jesus, so God, in Jesus, journeys with them. This is the beginning of discipleship. It is also the beginning of devotion. For both, all four of these elements are needed: God, Jesus, the Disciple and The Journey.

At times the journey with Jesus may lead you up a mount of transfiguration. At other times it will lead you to the door of a sick woman, to a wedding celebration, or to a life threatening storm, but at each moment it is Jesus who is Emmanuel. He is God with you, there to be turned to, to be quizzed with questions, to be nagged by doubts and to be listened to for his sometimes enigmatic guidance.

This is the journey of prayer. It is a pilgrimage that you take with God through this world, not just to God from this world. He is known not only in the quiet moments of withdrawal and retreat, but also in the general business of daily living. So it is here, in life's full richness of experience that you devote every task to him. You may be drawn aside, from time to time, for periods of special closeness, as the disciples were, but your relationship with God grows in <u>every</u> moment that you walk with him, not just these.

Spirituality, then, is a devotion to him in life and through life, not just in devotions.

\*\*\*\*\*

William Law, an Anglican priest at the beginning of the eighteenth century, saw the dangers of making the prayer life something separate from the rest of our living. His argument was that, "...there is no reason why we should make God the rule and measure of our prayers... and yet not make him the rule and measure of all the other actions of our life" (Devotional Classics, edited by Richard Forster & James Bryan Smith, Hodder & Stoughton Ltd., © 1993 Renovare, p280).

The answer, as he saw it, was to make life and prayer one action. To look completely to God in daily life, just as you look completely to him in prayer. The purpose of prayer then ceases to be a vehicle to carry you to God. Instead it becomes an affirmation of the presence of God and the rightful place of your desires, ways and purposes in relation to his. Then God will not only be a refuge from life, he will also be a source of strength in life.

Once you choose this particular railway line, spirituality becomes a pilgrimage you take with God through this world and not your flight to him out of this world. It is not living a life of devotions. It is the devotion of life as a living prayer for the closeness of God in every mundane and sublime moment.

Horatius Bonar wrote a hymn that expresses the simple beauty of this kind of spirituality. It begins with that deep desire within us all. When we strip away all the arguments and theological ramblings our minds sometimes take, this is what we find we have left: "Fill thou my life, O Lord my God in every part with praise, that my whole being may proclaim Thy being and thy ways." Until, in verses 3 and 6, we are finally led to a pilgrimage that is a continuous fellowship with God:

"Praise in the common things of life, its goings out and in;
Praise in each duty and each deed, however small and mean."
"So shall no part of day or night, from sacredness be free;
But all my life in every step, be fellowship with thee."

(Horatius Bonar, Hymns & Psalms 792, © 1983 Methodist Publishing House)

## CHAPTER 5

# THE RESOURCES OF THE NEAREST

In my discussions with other Christians about a possible model of spirituality which doesn't depend upon a daily quiet-time, one area of questioning kept recurring. "How would such a spirituality be fed and sustained, and how would it feed the Christian?" In other words, what are the spiritual resources for a form of spirituality which does not rely on a daily devotional habit? It is a good question, but one that needs to be asked of all devotional models. Let me explain what I mean by means of a short story or parable:

Mr Winkworth carefully tidied the box of six-inch nails on the corner of the shop counter to make sure that all the points were facing the same way; he liked to keep a tidy shop. It was an Aladdin's Cave type of emporium in which one felt that there really must be something one needed, if only one could find out what it was. The clank of the doorbell announced the arrival of another customer. The man, dragging behind him a grinning, but otherwise limp and lifeless figure, had that sort of pleading look that says, "I've lost the instructions and I'm not sure what to do."

"It's this Christian you sold me," He said, "It seems to have gone flat."

Mr Winkworth knew immediately what the most likely cause was, but he patiently examined the obviously useless Christian. He drew in a breath through pursed lips and looked up, "We haven't been giving it its quiet-time, have we, sir?" The customer gave him a puzzled look, as he had hoped, so he continued. "I'm afraid that these Christians must be put on charge every day or they never work properly. If they don't get their daily devotions, they just go flat, as you see." He gestured to the figure draped over the counter.

"I... I didn't... realise," the man flustered, "I mean, I did. Well, at least when I first got it I did, but you have to charge it up so early in the morning, and I have to get the kids ready for school and then I'm straight off to work and... " He looked at Mr Winkworth anxiously, "Isn't there anything you can do? It seems such a waste to just throw it away."

The shopkeeper's nod showed all the wisdom of accumulated experience. "Well," he said gravely, "We could put it on supercharge for you, sir, but it is a fairly expensive business. We have to send them off, either to the Power Christian Bible Week, or the Southermouth Retreat and Conference Centre, depending on the model." The customer sighed, "I'd like to give it a try." Mr Winkworth reached under the counter and pulled out his order book...

*****

It is easy to get the impression that the quality of our Christian life is precariously balanced on whether we have a quiet-time or not. There is what appears to be a seamless logic here, which goes something like this: The pattern of having daily devotional time periods is the Christian's main source of spiritual strength, because it is through the quiet-time that we are able to tune in to God and receive from him all that we need for the day. Therefore, without daily input, there is no spiritual sustenance, so the Christian will wither and die.

Various images are used to reinforce this line of thought. One classic illustration is that of an orchestra tuning up their instruments so that they can play in harmony with what the conductor commands. Another picture sees the performance of daily devotions as the Christian equivalent of the daily gathering of manna by the Israelites in the wilderness. Yet another illustration is the one that I have already alluded to in Mr Winkworth's tale, that of recharging our spiritual batteries.

They all have one common factor: they see daily devotions as our main spiritual resource for drawing from God that which we need to live a Christian life. Without them, therefore, we would spiritually starve, run down or be out of harmony with God's will. Which leaves us with the question that was set at the beginning of the chapter: if we do not have a regular daily quiet-time or devotional slot, how else can a Christian keep his relationship with God alive and growing?

For the first few years of my Christian life, the teaching I received left me in no doubt that my spiritual health rested entirely upon having a regular quiet-time. After hearing a few preachers, I had a suspicion that this razor edge may be even sharper than that. In the extreme, some Christian teaching goes on to suggest that your spiritual health actually depends upon the length of your quiet-time and even upon which version of the Bible you use. We are on dangerous ground if we start going down that route, after all, if five minutes of prayer is not enough, would ten minutes be, or twenty, or thirty?

Then there are the arguments about the type of prayers to use. Why, for instance, is free prayer supposed to better or more beneficial than those written by someone else, or the use of an aid like a rosary? In this way of thinking, whether or not you grow as Christian depends very precariously on making sure you get your devotions "right", because, obviously, "wrong" devotions will fail to be fully effective. Type "how to have an effective prayer life" into an internet search engine, and you'll see what I mean.

What is being said, in so many words, is that it is the quiet-time that keeps us close to God, and, therefore, it also keeps us open to receiving from him all that he has to give us. When a Christian has his devotions, some will say, they are "in the blessing" and God's blessings fall down on them like a golden shower... but not upon the one who hasn't had his quiet-time.

In my mind I have a picture of the poor Christian who hasn't done his devotions. He's the one at the prayer and praise meeting with his arms raised only halfway up and looking a bit forlorn because "the blessings" are falling down all around him whilst he is standing in a little dry patch.

Again, the logic appears to be seamless: those whose commitment to God is the deepest, who are serious about daily devotions, put themselves in a place where they are most likely receive God's blessings. They're the ones who will get a good drenching, whereas those who can only just manage to keep up to date with their daily notes will experience more of a lightish drizzle. Everyone else should only expect an occasional drip.

On the face of it, it does seem to make sense, but the more you think about it, the more it sounds as if dedicated good works are the payment being made in the hope of receiving something from God.

Not too long after becoming a Christian I began to feel that this 'hidden cost' was a little like a clever advertising con. I had had the introductory free package that goes with becoming a Christian, namely forgiveness and new life, but I got the impression that all the other promises of God, things like his presence, protection and guidance, the special features that we advertise as going with the Christian life, are actually optional extras, available only to those who can afford the supplementary payment of deep commitment.

We confidently tell people that all they need do to begin a new relationship with God is to put their trust in Jesus as Lord and Saviour, then, once we have them in the bag, we add the extra conditions; trust = commitment = an hour a day in prayer.

It is an equation that is a long way from the call to accept the Kingdom of Heaven as a little child accepts things. It is even further from the restored relationship of walking and talking with One who is with us in every stumbling step that we take along the Way.

It is not that having a quiet-time is intrinsically wrong, or that it cannot be fruitful and constructive. It is more that the inter-dependent association that has grown between the quiet-time and the presence of God can be misleading and create problems in the Christian's spirituality that should not exist. What this connection has done, in effect, is to turn personal devotions into a sort of spiritual good-luck charm.

In this way of thinking, not only should you not expect the blessings of the Christian life if you have not had your God slot, but you can also expect to be on our own if you have to face any obstacles that day. Consequently, the message is, "Beware lest you leave the house without having had a prayer time to shield you!"

On the other hand, if you have had your daily devotions you will be able stroll down the High Street without fear, knowing that a spiritual bubble protects you from the worst of life's woes. Of course, if this were true, it would be remarkably easy to spot those Christians who have not had their quiet-times. The next time you are at a fellowship meeting and one of the members is late because their boiler blew up, their house flooded, the plumber was late and the supplier didn't have the required spare part, you will know their hidden secret, *they haven't had their quiet-time.*

Or should you happen to find yourself in the slowest Post Office queue when you are already late for a doctor's appointment, double check to make sure that you had a prayer time that day. If you did, say a quick mental prayer for the person at the front of the queue as they are bound not to have had theirs.

The point that I am trying to make is that if the quality of the life we share with God depends on what kind of personal devotions we have then we are all in trouble... unless you can claim to have a perfect relationship with God. As I will discuss later, the degree of God's blessing on our lives ultimately depends on his grace, not on our own efforts to achieve them. Christianity is not a system of rewards and penalties. You should never think that God's blessing is given because you have done your spiritual duty for the day, and you should certainly never fear that his presence is withdrawn because you have not done it.

This is not just theological rhetoric with little or no bearing on practical, everyday Christian living. The reasons why you pray and what you think prayer does have a direct impact on how you perceive your relationship with God. They even affect your whole outlook on life and how you live out your faith from day to day.

This is something I had to discover for myself and have seen borne out in the experiences of others. One incident in particular caused me to begin re-thinking what devotions are all about: I was standing in the kitchen of a friend's house, helping their mum prepare the vegetables for dinner. It was their dad's day off, so he was in the garage attempting to mend something when there was a loud crash. Seconds later the back door flew open, dad rushed in, "Super-Glue, quick!" he shouted.

He then dived into the kitchen drawer and proceeded to do a very good impression of someone on the clothing stall at a jumble sale. Not finding the glue, he turned around to his wife, with the words "have you seen..." forming on his lips, but was cut off by the sight of the tube of glue swinging from her fingertips (how *do* they do that?).

He returned to the garage but reappeared a few minutes later, still very agitated. He looked around the kitchen, shook his head, rushed into the lounge and emerged a few moments later with a roll of sticky-tape.

This behaviour carried on for another half an hour, with dad obviously getting more and more agitated as whatever it was went from bad to worse. Finally the back door burst open, he stopped mid-flight across the room, and said, "I know what the matter is, I haven't had my quiet-time today." He promptly disappeared to his bedroom and re-emerged three-quarters of an hour later, once again in Christian mode.

Surely we are not so bound to the quiet-time that everything in the Christian's life hinges on or springs from it? If we are not, as I believe, then we are back with our starting question, which must be answered: "If our spirituality is not dependant on a daily devotional period, then where is our source of strength and sense of the presence of God to come from? What are the resources of The Nearest for those who walk with him?"

The standard teaching I was given about our relationship with God implied that being a Christian is a bit like being a cordless electric shaver. Daily usage tends to drain the power away so, to keep 'charged-up', we must plug into the power source for a few minutes every day, otherwise we run the risk of becoming run-down, powerless Christians.

My own cordless razor has a green light on it which blinks when it is fully powered-up and the instructions tell me that I should put it on charge for the recommended time period or until the light begins to flash. The same is true of us as Christians, the teaching goes, if we want to be really powered up, or simply function normally, then we must pray daily for as long as it takes to make that blinking light appear.

The trouble is, there are times when, for whatever reason, we cannot even see the blinking light. So we do the next best thing and try to 'power-up' for the recommended time period in the hope that it will at least keep the manufacturer's warranty in order.

In other words we peer blearily at the Bible for five minutes, nod off for five minutes, struggle to focus the brain to produce a few suitable prayer-type words and then spend the rest of the day feeling guilty that we haven't had a proper quiet-time.

As I've already pointed out, even if you have a time of devotion at some other time during the day, there can be other factors that have the same level of distraction from our focus on God. Added to all this is the nagging worry that if we are not plugged in properly, we will not get the full recharge we need – we will be underpowered Christians.

There are times when the busy-ness of life takes its toll on us and we find the need to recharge our physical and mental resources. In the same way we also feel the need to rekindle the inner spiritual flame occasionally through special times of dedicated devotion. This, though, makes no difference to the nearness of God, only to our awareness of it.

We are alive to God just as we are alive to life, and live in his presence. That life is God given not quiet-time given.

The truth is, there is actually no such thing as a Cordless Christian. We all come with cords attached and are therefore permanently plugged in to the power source. From the point of view of the New Testament, if we are not plugged in to the power source then we do not work at all. Galatians 2:20 says, "I have been crucified with Christ, and I no longer live, but Christ lives in me..."

Similarly in Romans 8:10, 11: "But if Christ is in you, your body is dead because of sin, yet your spirit is alive because of righteousness. And if the Spirit of him who raised Jesus from the dead is living in you, he who raised Christ from the dead will also give life to your mortal bodies through his Spirit who lives in you."

Many Christians are being deceived into thinking their relationship with God is second-class because their quiet-times are second-class. Whether or not you have a daily devotional habit, personal devotions should never be seen as a charge-up period to keep you going, whilst you spend the rest of the day detached from God and "running down".

You are not cordless, you are permanently plugged in.

This simple truth is at the heart of what being a Christian is all about. This is the true and real blessing of being with The Nearest. If you truly want to find complete freedom in our walk with God, embrace and learn this one fact, because when you do, suddenly his presence with you is released from the confines of a few minutes of prayer to being here with you in every living moment.

Jesus urged his followers to think of their relationship with God in this way by using an image that the people of his time would have clearly understood. He said, "I am the vine; you are the branches. If a man remains in me and I in him, he will bear much fruit; apart from me you can do nothing. If anyone does not remain in me, he is like a branch that is thrown away and withers" John 15:5-6.

Just as it is impossible to think of a vine branch living, let alone bearing fruit, apart from the vine, so it is inconceivable to think of ourselves as being somehow detachable from him – together we are vine and branches. They are not two separate entities with some loose connection between them.

It is his Spirit within that makes us alive to God and without him we have no life. Understanding this should be a fundamental principle of spirituality and ought to shape the way we approach prayer and devotion.

Let me give another illustration from modern life. If you connect to the internet through broadband, the chances are you will have a router or similar box which feeds stuff from the web onto your computer. There are two types of routers: wireless and wired. The wireless router 'beams' information from the internet onto your computer via radio waves, giving you the ability to wander out into the garden with your laptop and surf the web from there. The problem with wireless routers is that the further you wander from the router, the weaker the signal gets, until eventually it is lost altogether.

Exchange the words "internet" for "God" and "router" for

"prayer", and you get a common teaching about how prayer works. You keep connected to God, it is sometimes said, by staying close to him in prayer, let your focus on your prayer life wander and you 'lose the signal'. Wander too far and you may lose your connection altogether.

The other kind of router, the wired one, is exactly what it says. Your computer is permanently connected to the router with a wire. The disadvantage is obvious; you can never be further than a cable's length from your router. The advantage, though, is that you are permanently connected to the internet and your signal is always full strength.

It's actually the *wired* router which more closely represents the nature of your relationship to God and prayer. You can't lose your connection. Whether you surf once a day for twenty minutes or connect only briefly at odd moments throughout the day makes no difference to the quality of your connection to the Web. It's always full strength.

*****

In a small valley not far from Bristol, there are some ancient lead mines. They have been used at various periods of time throughout human history, and because of that the countryside around was scarred with the open cast mines and the land poisoned by the slag heaps. Many of these still lie bare of nature's attempts to re-colonise them. In the middle of this man-made landscape there is a natural spring. It bubbles up out of the ground endlessly, bringing water into the valley and, all around its banks, life is flourishing.

The power of that little spring is deceptive. It was probably there before the Romans were. It has managed to force its way up through the tons of debris that have collapsed upon it over the centuries. Somehow it has managed to carve its way through the destruction that humanity has caused around it, and wherever it flows life has taken hold in an abundance of flowering greenery.

Believe it or not, Jesus didn't say to the Samaritan woman by the well, "I am The Stand-pipe, and if anyone pumps hard enough when they come to me, they might just get a drip out of me, but they had better be prepared to put in the effort." Instead he said, "Whoever drinks the water I give him will never thirst. Indeed, the water I give him will become in him a spring of water welling up to eternal life" (John 4:14).

Jesus is not a tap that you turn on whenever you next feel spiritually thirsty. He is an eternal spring of life within you, flowing from the heart of God. The landscape around you may seem barren and the stream hard to find, but the spring cannot dry up. It is always still there, even if it is temporarily buried under piles of slag and debris.

The contrast in the story of the Samaritan woman is quite clearly between the constant strenuous work that is required to get a bucketful of water and the endlessly flowing refreshment that comes from a bubbling spring.

Jesus was sitting by a well at the time and using it as an illustration of the difference between physical refreshment and the deeper spiritual refreshment he could offer. What he was offering, he said, was not a source that had to be gone back to again and again, day after day, like the well water that only had a temporary power to quench the thirst one bucketful at a time. Instead, what he gives you is a source within, a residing and constant spring of refreshment. He is the spring within your soul, just as he is the life in your veins.

The Old Testament paints a very similar picture of our relationship with God in Psalm 1:1-3. A person who delights in God's will, it says, is like a tree planted by streams of water. According to my concordance, the Hebrew word for "streams" in this verse is PELEG, a word that indicates, as I understand it, man-made irrigation channels rather than natural watercourses.

In the arid climate of Israel riverbeds were often dry through long months of the year, but when the rains came, they often flash-flooded, carrying vast quantities of the much needed water away. To make sure that their fields got the water they needed, farmers would cut irrigation channels into the land. These were damned up in various places so that the flow of water could be controlled and diverted to every corner of the field.

A tree planted by these irrigation channels would be in a place most likely to receive water in the rainy season and be able to reach down to the water held below the surface. Even in the dry season, its leaves would still be green.

As rain was considered to be a blessing from God, these irrigation channels were, in some ways, regarded literally as channels of his blessing.

Psalm 1 is saying that those who delight in and thirst for God's will are blessed because, like the tree planted by an irrigation channel, they are in the place most likely to receive God's blessing. It is a powerful image of spirituality. We are not to think of ourselves as potted palms, isolated from a source of water and therefore in need of regular trips to the well to be watered. As long as that thirst for God, that "delight in the Lord", is there, we are trees planted where our taproots permanently reach down into the water table.

All forms of personal devotion, like the surface water in these arid regions, are seasonal. Times of flowing abundance are interspersed with times of drought. From our point of view, the dry seasons of prayer make it appear as though the source of living water has dried up altogether, and it feels as though desiccation threatens to draw out from us every drop of spiritual life.

In dry seasons, some trees, as a strategy for survival, drop their leaves and sometimes even whole branches. To all outward appearances they look as if they are dying, however it is just the equivalent of autumn when a tree can rest from its growth and lose diseased branches.

As long as that thirst and longing for God is there, the dry period is not so much a season of death but a time of dormancy from surface growth, an interval when the roots can reach down beyond the dust and the heat to discover a deeper source of the water that gives life, perhaps for the first time.

One of the less helpful, almost misleading images that is sometimes given to illustrate the need for a quiet-time, likens the daily prayer to the act of tuning in a radio to particular station. We need that time of prayer at the beginning of the day, the argument goes, in order to tune in to God's wavelength and so be enabled to hear his voice and thus more clearly find his guidance through the day.

The first question I want to ask of the illustration is why sleep should put our spiritual antennae out of tune. Also, I am in no doubt that we should not see our reception of God's voice as something that is dependent upon the preciseness and length of time spent "tuning in".

If anything, we are on a pre-set frequency. After all, didn't Jesus say, "My sheep listen to my voice"? (John 10:27). With one exception, the radio image is not a very helpful one, and I would rather we abandon it as an image of prayer altogether. The exception is to say that the hearing of God's voice is not so much dependent on our being in tune, but whether or not we have the radio on at all. Any type of prayer is more like turning on a radio that is already pre-set to the God channel.

Let's go back to the sheep for a minute. It always amazes me, when I see a field full of ewes with their lambs that, in all that baaing and bleating, the lambs are still able to find their own mothers. To my ears all I can hear is "baa!" If I were to listen really hard I might detect a few variations in pitch, but each lamb obviously hears his own mother's voice quite distinctly from all the others. This ability to distinguish one voice clearly out of a thousand others is, I am sure, not a property that is unique only to sheep. It is not for nothing that Jesus said, "My sheep listen to my voice."

When there are a thousand voices clamouring for our attention, we worry that we will not be able to pick out the voice of God from among them. And yet Jesus seems to be saying that when he speaks, his voice is distinctive. "So why is his voice not clear to me?" every Christian shouts, upon reading that verse.

The sound of that voice must be learned, just as any young creature must learn the voice of its mother. We also need to be careful about exactly what we mean by the voice of God, something that I will deal with later.

Listening for God's voice is much more than pinning your ears back for clearly spoken words – which is not to say that might not happen. The point is that acquiring an ear for the voice of the shepherd is not something that can be forced. It is something that develops, as we grow closer to him. Anyone with children will tell you that they have the amazing ability not to hear at certain times, usually when it's time to come in from playing with friends.

From the parent's point of view, there is a big difference between being heard and being listened to. So the aim of all devotion is not so much the hearing of but the listening to the Shepherd's voice.

The point of all this is to make it clear that in your life with God it is not any system of devotions or pattern of spiritual discipline that is the source of your spiritual strength; it is God, who is always near. When God is near, when we know his closeness, no other resource is needed. He is the Source of all and the Resource for all. It is, as it says in Psalm 23, "The Lord is my shepherd, I shall not be in want."

# CHAPTER 6

# THE NEAREST IN THE WILDERNESS

I have always liked survival stories. There is something in them that is both inspiring and at the same time challenging. They show so clearly the resourcefulness of the human spirit, but I have always found myself wondering whether I would cope as well in the same circumstances.

In the summer of 1972 the Robertson family were sailing their yacht around the Pacific Ocean when killer whales attacked it. The boat sank in minutes. There was no time to take a compass, charts, or other essential equipment. They scrambled aboard an inflatable life raft and managed to store just three days' worth of food and water in a little dinghy, which they kept in tow.

It was not long before their food ran out, the life raft sank and they had to cram themselves into the dinghy. Somehow their inventiveness and strength of character enabled them to survive for thirty-seven days before finally being rescued. It is an amazing, inspiring and true story that Dougal Robertson writes about in his book, "Survive the Savage Sea."

Now let me tell you about St Anthony: Anthony was born in AD 251 and was the son of wealthy Egyptian parents. When they died he inherited their fortune and looked set to be comfortable and prosperous for the rest of his life. One day he heard the teaching of Jesus. The text being preached on was Matthew 19:21, "If you want to be perfect, go, sell your possessions and give to the poor, and you will have treasure in heaven." For Anthony, it was as if Jesus was speaking directly to him. Incredibly, he immediately gave away his entire family fortune, with the exception of an amount to ensure that his sister was looked after.

In those days it was common practice for those seeking closeness God to live on the outskirts of their town or community, free from the distractions of everyday life. At first this is what Anthony did, choosing to live the life of an ascetic in an old tomb and dedicating himself to prayer and fasting. Here, according to tradition, he faced spiritual warfare, literally fighting demons which often appeared in the form of wild beasts that physically attacked him.

After about fifteen years he felt the need to withdraw from society altogether, so he crossed the Nile and found a deserted fort near Pispir (now Der el Memum). He lived there for another twenty years, his only contact with other people being the food that was thrown to him over the castle walls.

As people heard about what Anthony was doing, they travelled to find him and learn about the kind of spirituality he was seeking. In time a small community of pilgrims and disciples built up around the fort and Anthony was called upon to give them teaching and guidance.

At first he refused, but they kept on begging for instruction in how to live a spiritual life and so eventually Anthony appeared. They were expecting a withered and wizened man, starved by the years of frugality, but instead they were faced with a figure who was fit and vibrant. So Anthony began to teach them about the rewards of living an ascetic lifestyle devoted to prayer.

For Anthony, though, seeking God meant suffering the hardships of the desert as well as living in seclusion, so he retreated even further into the desert, between the Nile and the Red Sea, where he lived out his remaining years.

Although there were other Christian ascetics living in the desert in the third century, Anthony was the one who became famous as the first of what came to be called "The Desert Fathers." They were the inspiration for monasticism, which followed their example of setting themselves apart from society and living an austere life as a means of showing devotion and achieving a deeper spirituality. For them physical suffering and self-denial were an integral part of devotion and the key to unlocking a closer and richer relationship with God.

What these two stories have in common is their portrayal of human survival in the wilderness. Yet it is where they differ that is more relevant, especially when we start thinking about them as analogies for how we can survive those periods in our lives that are like a spiritual wilderness. And the difference lies in the simple matter of choice.

The Robertson family had their wilderness experience thrust upon them. Other than accepting death, there were no other options open to them except to summon up every ounce of courage and ingenuity in order to just survive.

Although Anthony felt the compelling call of God to enter the desert, he still had the choice: to obey or not. For him, suffering the hardships of the wilderness was something to be deliberately chosen and then embraced as the means to his end – deeper spirituality.

One thing we learn from the Robertson's experience is what the definition of a wilderness is. It doesn't have to be rocks and sand to be a desert. A desert is just an environment that is alien and hostile to us, and where we either do not know how to find the essentials for life, or where they are scarce.

As it turns out, this is also quite a good definition of what a wilderness experience is in a relationship with God.

Firstly, it is not just a dry patch in your devotions, although the two things do sometimes coincide. Secondly, it is not those times when the circumstances of life are difficult - they happen to non-Christians too. Instead the wilderness experience occurs when you feel that all the resources that you depend upon for spiritual life and nourishment appear to have utterly evaporated around you.

Even if you cannot identify with what this might be like in

the extreme, it should not be too difficult to understand how there might be periods in your life when prayer becomes a deep struggle; when you find yourself in a barren spiritual landscape where you feel lost and isolated. In times like this, it seems as if God is remote, somewhere outside and beyond this desert that is now void of any spiritual meaning for you.

In this wilderness you may find that the only way you know how to pray ceases to have significance or, worse, is taken away from you altogether. Christian activities which were once nourishing and uplifting now have a sense of futility about them. In the absence of being able to find any meaningful way to approach God, you arrive at a place in this desert where all that you have left is your existence. You know you exist and that *maybe* God might exist... somewhere.

So it is, in those times of nothingness, that realization dawns upon how conventional teaching about prayer and devotion assumes that you are always able to offer it. When it becomes difficult or even impossible to perform the acts of devotion, as we normally understand them, there is little left with which to replace them. You are simply expected to survive your way through the desert and generally, our response is to take one of three courses of action:

1 Flight
This is where we do anything we can to escape. The alien environment we find ourselves in has a way of making us feel vulnerable and there is a compelling urge to try and get back to familiar ground. The normal sources of spiritual refreshment have dried up and the temptation is to look for God outside our current circumstances, because wherever he is, he doesn't appear to be anywhere here.

In effect, our response is to try to change our location in order to find God. We change the way we pray, think about moving churches, look for an answer in our health or diet, or do any number of things to change our circumstances in some way.

## 2 Self-pity

This is otherwise known as PLOM Syndrome (poor little old me). Helplessness in the wilderness can easily lead to hopelessness. We feel that we are in a situation not of our own making and there doesn't appear to be any way out. We feel sorry for ourselves and blame God (or sometimes the devil) for our circumstances. After all, God is omnipotent isn't he? So, why doesn't he do something about our predicament?

This time our response is to turn inward and change our attitude towards God. Instead of being the object of our love, he becomes the object of our anger and frustration. We do not particularly care about God, all we know is that it is his fault we are here and if he wants us to get out of the wilderness, he can do it himself.

## 3 The hero/martyr response

This is where, if we were in a Hollywood film, we would be the wounded actor who, clutching a bleeding leg says, "Just leave me, save yourselves." We adopt the martyr role. Whatever the difficulty or problem it is that we are facing, our reaction is the God-is-teaching-me-a-lesson approach.

God must have placed us in the desert for a purpose, we tell ourselves, so we must stay in the desert and until we have discovered whatever that lesson is.

We throw ourselves into suffering the hardships of the wilderness, as if they are the whole purpose for being there. We conclude that perhaps if we are more patient, or more pious, or more prayerful, less sinful etc our time in the wilderness might end.

In other words, our response in this instance is to try to

change ourselves in order to find God.

Ultimately, none of these responses to the wilderness is particularly helpful, but there is a fourth response to an encounter with the wilderness, one that we see in the life of Jesus, in the account of his temptations in the desert.

I think we sometimes get fixed on the idea that the purpose of Jesus' time in the desert was to overcome temptation and fight evil. Fundamentally, Jesus' wilderness experience was a time when his own spiritual identity and his relationship with God were being challenged. When you take the temptations as a whole you begin to see that the real temptation for Jesus was to become someone he wasn't supposed to be – a ruler of earthly kingdoms, subject only to the devil. In other the words, the devil was trying to get Jesus to change how he felt about himself, his circumstance and God.

This leads us to one inevitable conclusion, to a more constructive and helpful way through the wilderness: be yourself. At first glance that sounds trite and simplistic, but I hope to show that it is actually a much more profound answer that it seems.

If you find yourself lost in the desert, one of the first pieces of advice you hear from survival experts is to stay where you are (unless you know the way out with absolute certainty). The same general rule applies in the spiritual desert, except that "stay where you are" becomes just "be who you are."

All of which brings me to some bad news. You may have been reading this chapter hoping to find the secret to escaping from your own particular set of circumstances. Unfortunately I cannot tell you how to get out of your particular desert. The wilderness encounter, if you should have to face it, is a life changing experience and there are as many different ways of dealing with it as there are people who experience it. What I can tell you is that every way out of the desert begins by first finding God *in* the desert, and that the only way out of the wilderness is to walk through it, with God.

Redundancy, retirement, unemployment, illness, bereavement, children growing up, being trapped in a seemingly hopeless situation; the wilderness encounter can happen for many reasons and in varying degrees. Although you enter the desert by many roads, the experience of it is invariably the same.

Everything you once relied on is stripped away from you. You find yourself with nothing left but your existence. All the things that you have surrounded yourself with, the things that used to give your life meaning and direction, become just more rocks in the desert. Something in you wants more. You find yourself asking the most fundamental questions of all: Why am I here? What is my purpose? Where is God? Who is God?

You might be tempted to answer the questions by looking for your purpose at it relates to others. You see a purpose for yourself in your job, your vocation, your calling, in leisure activities, in supporting your partner, or in your place in your church or community.

Looked at this way, it's not too difficult to see how easy it is for people to lose their sense of identity and purpose in difficult circumstances.

That was a crucial part of Jesus' own experience in the desert. He was tempted to see himself as a ruler of all the kingdoms of earth. What had to come out of it, for Jesus, was an understanding of his own identity and purpose as it related to God, which was completely different to that which the wilderness was trying to tell him.

The bottom line is that surviving in the wilderness is about being in God. That is, just learning to be in God.

The question that all our efforts at Spirituality are trying to answer is, "What does it mean to be who we are in God?"

When you find yourself in the wilderness it is precisely who you are and what your life is about that is being challenged, sometimes to the very core of your being, and you are brought back to the most fundamental question of all, "What am I here for?"

Whether or not you believe that the account of the creation of Adam and Eve in Genesis is a factual and historical record makes no difference to the theological point that is being made. As I mentioned in chapter three, the human race was made for a perfect, very special kind of relationship with God. The setting for this relationship is the Garden of Eden, which, throughout the Bible, is virtually synonymous with the presence of God. (Genesis 3, Ezekiel 28:11*ff*, Ezekiel 31, 1 Corinthians 3:9, Revelation 2:7, Isaiah 51:3) To walk in the Garden, as Adam and Eve did, is to walk in God's presence and favour.

Eden was their world, but it was also their Garden of Encounter with God. In other words, their world was the place where they expected to meet God (more about this later). It is important to understand that Adam and Eve are there as proto-types or ideal models for the whole human race. So one way of looking at this passage is to see that we have been made to exist in the presence of God, or more specifically, we are purpose built for a relationship with God – this is the meaning of life.

In Genesis chapter three verse eight we are given a hint of what this relationship is supposed to be like. We read how the man and the woman were walking around in the garden in the cool of the evening breeze in the presence of God. The picture that is painted here is of a natural, easy relationship in which Adam and Eve simply walked and talked with God as the third person there with them.

Their lives are quite literally laid bare before him, there is nothing to hide. It is this relationship that has been lost to us. After Adam and Eve choose to sidestep God's authority, every-thing changes. Their relationship with God is compromised, he becomes distant from them and concealment replaces the openness of before. Even if you don't believe in the doctrine of the fall, the pattern of a broken, imperfect relationship in need of restoration and fulfilment is still valid.

Sermons on the subject of salvation so often tend to focus on what you have been saved from (_from_ sin and _from_ evil), but it is what you have been saved _for_ that is truly astounding. You have been saved for exactly this kind of relationship with God; a relationship where you exist in him and where your whole being is taken up in his, because it is this for which you were created.

The main purpose of Jesus' act of salvation then, is to not the destruction of sin or the offering of forgiveness, these are the means to the end. Jesus' life, death, resurrection and ascension all happened to restore the lost nearness of God to the human race.

*****

I wonder sometimes whether we spend too much time thinking about how to get rid of the imperfections from our lives instead of concentrating on how to cultivate this natural relationship with God. One thing that Adam and Eve show us very clearly, as long as we are walking in the Garden, we will know when we have overstepped the mark... we will find ourselves searching for a bush to hide behind.

God knows who we are and his primary purpose for us is to be who we are in him. Even in non-Christian contexts you hear quite a lot about being yourself and accepting yourself, sometimes in sentimental ways that are little more than platitudes. And yet, underneath the sentimentality there lies an important truth - the knowledge that God loves us for who we are and comes to us where we are.

For this to have any real meaning for us or make any impact on our lives, we need to go further. This truth must be balanced with the knowledge that God also calls us forward, to become more like the whole person he created us to be. After all, it stands to reason that, unless you are perfect, there are changes God wants to make in your life.

You should not be frightened by this. These changes are not a threat to your identity, to make you into something that you are not, just the opposite, in fact. He wants to free you to be who you really are; to fulfil in you the person he made you to be. He sees so clearly what is _you_ in what you do and think. He also knows what comes from the child within, from the child that still needs to grow up in him. He knows what actions and thoughts are motivated by the insecurities and inner hurts which you have locked away through a lifelong habit of protecting your vulnerability.

It is Psalm 139 again.

"O Lord, you have searched me and you know me.
You know when I sit and when I rise;
You perceive my thoughts from afar.
You discern my going out and my lying down;
You are familiar with all my ways.
Before a word is on my tongue you know it completely,
     O Lord."

When God looks at you in this way, with such complete love of your entire being, what is expected in return is not that you then try to be someone else. What God hopes for and works in you for, above all other things, is that you be yourself, with all your quirks and flaws, in him.

It has to be this way, simply because it is only by being yourself completely that you are able to offer God complete devotion from yourself. All the same, how often do you subconsciously try to match yourself up to that image of the model Christian you hold in your mind's eye?

Psalm 139 makes it so clear that God knows what motivates your every thought and action, and that there is nothing that you can hide behind. This is not intended to frighten you. It is meant to be a source of comfort and hope, because it means that God knows why you do things you do. He knows what it is that prevents from you loving him completely. He can see, as if they were a glow-in-dark, yellow safety jacket, the secret motivations and unconscious reasoning that you keep even from yourself, and yet still he gazes upon you with complete loving attention.

If God, knowing all that can be known about you, still delights in you and embraces you, how much more loved and accepted can you be?

I began this chapter by talking about the wilderness experience and how it has the capacity to strip our lives down to barest essentials. When all the theology, doctrine, ritual and tradition are stripped away from religion, what is left at the end is our divine purpose: We are "To Be" in God.

Although you cannot always see it at the time, an encounter with the wilderness will ultimately help you define yourself in relation to God.

You exist in God, but this is also your purpose in life, which implies, amazingly, that your reason for existence is also his greatest gift to you, the gift of existence in the heart of God.

This must be the starting point in all your explorations of spirituality and what it means to live a devoted life. "To be" for The Nearest is the beginning and foundation of all devotion, because it can only be devotion when it comes from who you are.

## CHAPTER 7

# SERVING THE NEAREST

### Service As A Role

I want to tell you about one or two remarkable people with
equally remarkable ministries that I have met on my Christian
pilgrimage: Violet's ministry was a ministry of greetings cards.

I helped out in a Christian bookshop for a while and I had not
been there for too long before I noticed the same woman kept
coming into the shop at least once a week to buy cards. At first I
just thought she had lots of relatives and friends with whom she
liked to keep in touch. It turned out that most of the cards she
bought were for people that she had heard about who were ill,
bereaved, housebound or simply just in need of a little encouragement.

So she bought them cards.

She would spend a long time carefully choosing each one,
looking for the right pictures and words to fit the need.

Then there are Dora and Ian. Their ministry quite simply is
generosity. They are the most generous people I have ever met.
They have a way of giving that makes you feel that you received
something more than whatever it is they want you to have. From
them I have learned that generosity has absolutely nothing to do
with the quantity, frequency or quality of gifts.

I don't know how they do it, but when you have received
something from Dora and Ian there is no embarrassment or
feeling of awkwardness that you sometimes get when people
give you something that you know cannot be repaid. Instead you
feel they have managed to turn giving into a sacrament, so that

it is as if a touch of God comes through what they have given – even when what they have given might be just their time or friendship.

Or I could tell you about the person whom my wife calls "The Angel." The angel sings in the choir. It is not that her singing is in any way more proficient than other singers or that her voice has a unique quality, although she is very good, it is just that when she sings you feel blessed.

And there are others that I could add to the list: Dancers that have preached sermons to me without saying a word, flower arrangers who are to be able display the glory of God, people with a gift for administration that goes way beyond good management, not to mention the people whose cake baking, tea making, welcomes, smiles or reading genuinely add significantly to the life, wellbeing and fellowship of the Church.

None of these people have been to theological college. They do not wear a dog-collar and they have never had the public recognition of having had hands lain upon them, but there is no doubt in my mind that they exercise very real ministries, every bit as valid and important as any member of the clergy. It is quite right that we recognise before the Church those whom we call ministers, deacons, priests etc, but we also need to affirm that there are no classes of ministry. It is something that belongs to every Christian, however poverty stricken they feel of faith, spirituality or gifts. Service of God is a part of what it means to be a follower of Jesus.

I told you earlier about my disastrous attempt to instigate a revival after having read the biography of Smith Wigglesworth. That day I discovered two things: firstly, that I wasn't an evangelist; my gifts and talents lie in other directions; secondly, I discovered that I couldn't generate something that wasn't a part of who I was.

A deep desire to love and serve God cannot be just 'put on'. Just as artists can only express in their art what is within them to create, so, in precisely the same way, Christian devotion and service have to come from within who we are.

Christian life and service can never be thought of as role-play. The reason I say this is because it is something we occasionally fall prey to.

We hold in our minds an ideal of what we feel our praying ought to be like. We also think we know what our life ought to be like if it were wholly lived for God. Whether or not these are realistic models is another question, but have you noticed how these ideals are _always_ different from where we believe we are at the moment. If we are not careful, what can happen is that we try to realign our lives to fit that role.

I am convinced this is because we all hold, somewhere in our subconscious, a sort of "model Christian." It probably comes from a distillation of all the sermons and teaching that we have ever heard, explaining what the ideal Christian life should be like. It is a bit like those cut-out figures in children's comics or craft books. There was a blank figure and various clothes with little tabs on that you had to cut out and fold over the figure. In the same way, we hear a sermon on how prayer should work, another about the ideal way to study the Bible, a further one on the need for miracle-working faith and we pin these together onto our idea of what a Christian is. Then we look in the mirror and realize we don't quite match up to the cardboard cut-out.

Having such models is not necessarily a bad thing, because it stops you being complacent and give you goals to work towards - when the models are realistic. If, on the other hand, you do not see them for what they are, as ideals, and at the same time you feel yourself to be spiritually weak or vulnerable, you might easily think that approaching God involves a change from who you are towards that cardboard cut-out.

There is a hymn that expresses simply but powerfully the yearning prayer that we find ourselves praying from time to time:

"Dear Master, in whose life I see
All that I would but fail to be,
Let thy clear light forever shine,
To shame and guide this life of mine.

Though what I dream and what I do
In my weak days are always two,
Help me oppressed by things undone,
O thou, whose deeds and dreams were one!"

John Hunter (1848-1917), Hymns and Psalms, ©1983 The Methodist Publishing House.

God wants us *to be* with him. This is the definition of our existence; to seek to be who we are and do all that we do, in God's presence.

All of human life is encompassed within these two spheres of being and doing.

From our point of view, being and doing appear to have quite different characteristics, involving quite different states of mind. "Being" we think of as something that is largely passive, whilst "doing" necessarily involves activity. Therefore it is also natural to conclude that they have very little in common and you cannot exist in both spheres at the same time. After all, it is impossible to be both passive and active at the same, isn't it?

It might be that it is because we see them this way that being and doing are frequently separated, or at least addressed distinctively, when we talk about spirituality. Even when they are not regarded as distinct, it is quite common to find that being is raised in stature above doing as the more worthy or more spiritual pursuit. In fact some even go further and say that, of the two, being is the only one which relates to spirituality. It is a value judgement that is often illustrated with the Mary and Martha analogy mentioned in chapter two.

Mary, of whom Jesus says, "Mary has chosen what is best", is understood as the embodiment of being. Therefore, we conclude, living a life of prayer and meditation must be "better" than living in the busy-ness and activity of the world. Conversely, the normal activity of daily life is not regarded as a spiritual a pursuit, in the proper sense, and is seen at best as a distraction to true spirituality. By implication, it seems we can only conclude that we should regard work, home life and even leisure activities as a distraction to devotion. What was I saying earlier about the influence of monasticism on spirituality? Be honest now, how often have you thought that you would be a more spiritual person if only the things of everyday life didn't get in the way?

We have even given names to the being and doing spheres of existence:  Everything we normally think as the non-religious daily life of human affairs we call "secular"; whereas all that we regard as religious is largely labelled as "sacred."

Now here's a funny thing: The Oxford English Dictionary defines sacred as, "2 religious rather than secular." (Concise Oxford English Dictionary, Tenth Edition, Revised, © Oxford University Press 2002) OK... so we have to define sacred by our understanding of what it means to be secular. And yet when we look at the dictionary's definition of what secular is we read this; "adj. 1 not religious, sacred or spiritual." (ibid) Err...what? Actually, the dictionary does expand the definitions further (barely though). Even so, what is made clear by the definitions is that "religious" and "secular" should be thought of as virtual polar opposites.

We have come to regard "religious" and "secular" in the same way and this has led us to separate our lives into two spheres: there is the sphere of sacred, religious, _spiritual,_ things and the sphere of secular, worldly, _unspiritual_ things.

Take, for instance, the way in which The Kingdom and The World are talked about in Christian circles as though they were mutually exclusive spheres, if not opposites. As a consequence we tend to see these two spheres of life rather like the circles on the Olympic flag, nearly separate, just overlapping but always distinct.

The result of this division is a kind of split spirituality in which we find ourselves trying to live in two modes of thinking and acting. We see "being" as something that we do *with* God (prayer, devotion etc.). "Doing", on the other hand, encompasses daily life and all those deeds we do in service *for* God.

If you begin with this notion, then you are led naturally to the conclusion that the spiritual sphere is an area of our life that requires movement from wherever we are to enter into wherever it is. (How often have you heard people talk about moving into or going into prayer?) The result of this is that we see the Christian life as being spent going backwards and forwards between the two modes of spiritual and secular life. So the idea that prayer is the means for moving between the two realms is reinforced. When we feel we have spent too long in the secular, doing sphere, we feel the need to draw aside and, through prayer, enter the being sphere where we can be close to God for a while.

In reality the Christian life cannot be differentiated this clearly. For one thing, we describe prayer as an action that we perform as a part of life, so prayer, even contemplative prayer, is clearly something that we do. At the same time we also recognise that many of the things we do are, in fact, expressions of prayer. Who we are within is naturally expressed in what we do without, so there is a blurring of the boundaries between being and doing.

Ideally, all that we are and all that we do is taken up within God and so living for and serving God are interwoven with who we are. In reality though, we are so heavily programmed into looking at life from these two points of view, the secular and the sacred, that we find it almost impossible not to think about them as separate, albeit interrelated, ways of living, thinking, being and doing.

We make connections between the two modes of being and doing in a variety of ways, but if we use two circles as models for them, three broad categories emerge illustrating how we understand and put them into practice.

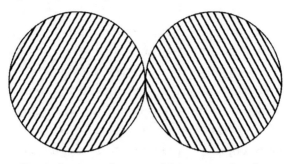

Fig 1. Separate but touching on each other

Fig 2. Overlapping with some commonality

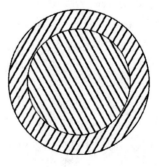

Fig 3. One contained within the other

In all three instances the two circles are regarded as distinct, though always related, spheres of life. All the same, all three models are inadequate for a life-encompassing model of spirituality, specifically because this differentiation between secular and sacred is, in reality, an artificial one. There just is no compartmentalisation in our lives. Spirituality is a part of who we are and cannot be separated off from the rest of our lives anymore than our love or sense of humour could be.

If we have a model of spirituality that addresses only some aspects of our whole being, we are effectively denying a part of our nature to God, because what we do is tied inextricably together with who we are. Both must be expressed in our spirituality and in the forms we use to express it. We are encouraged to set aside time and prayer to focus on being; ought we not do the same for doing?

There is a fourth way of looking at this relationship between being and doing which doesn't split us up into separate compartments.

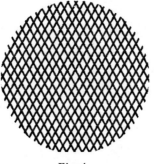

Fig.4

Now things look a little different.

There are no longer two separate spheres, just one interwoven whole. Note also that there are no boundaries on this model. There is no split personality divided between secular and spiritual. These distinctions have gone; instead there is just a wholeness of being and doing.

We see this supremely in the life of Jesus and it is expressed in the second verse of John Hunter's hymn.

"Though what I dream and what I do
In my weak days are always two,
Help me oppressed by things undone,
O thou, whose deeds and dreams were one!"

In other words, who Jesus was and what he did were fused together as one. His relationship with God was displayed perfectly in his ministry to the world. It is impossible to think about what Jesus did without, at the same time, thinking about who he was. So for us, both who we are and what we do must somehow be bound together in our relationship with God and the forms we use to express it.

One of the reasons we tend to separate life into sacred and secular is because we tend to think of "being" and "doing" as synonyms for "praying" and "serving". We regard prayer as something that comes from within the core of who we are and the means by which we draw strength and inspiration from God in order to go (there's that idea of movement again) and serve him. The act of serving God is subsequently seen as the way in which our spiritual reserves are drained from us, requiring us to return to prayer to recharge the spiritual batteries.

This thought probably didn't come from any one individual or movement, more likely it evolved through the history of the Church. As its status and power grew in the middle ages so the phrase "The Church" began to be associated with the Church as an establishment, rather than a community of believers (remember that separate denominations didn't really exist in those days).

In time the priesthood became an acceptable, almost fashionable, vocation. In a similar way in which people talk about joining the army nowadays, so people talked about

"Going into the Church." The Church, and the way of life associated with it, was regarded as something separate from and different to the normal daily life everyone else was living.

These changes were reflected within church architecture and even the furnishings used. What went on at the altar was regarded as too holy for common or uninitiated people to see and so large screens called rood screens were erected to separate the altar area from the nave, where the laity sat.

In turn, this was based on the Holy of Holies found in the temple of the Old Testament, where the sanctuary of the altar was regarded as so holy that only a properly consecrated priest might approach it. And in fact "The Holy of Holies" has even been used as a model for prayer, as the sanctuary you go into away from the rest of the world to find God.

In addition, daily life in the middle ages was hard for most people. It took all a person's time and effort to sustain a living. Prayer in the home was rare until much later (possibly not even until reformation). Therefore, churches became the place where one went to pray and to take refuge from the graft of daily life. It is not difficult to see how the concept of "secular" as distinct from "spiritual" or "sacred" began to develop.

This has so strongly coloured the way we think about religion that for many people this is the church's sole purpose. The whole point of going to church once a week, as they see it, is to get away from the daily grind, to get away from the world and be refreshed in the presence of God.

The secular/spiritual distinction has become so much a part of the way we traditionally think about prayer and service that it all sounds completely logical. Our daily lives, for the most part, do not feel particularly religious or spiritual, and yet some of the things Jesus taught actually point us in a different direction.

He was asked once what he thought the greatest commandment was and at first glance the answer he gave doesn't quite make grammatical sense, but it does make absolute spiritual sense. He answered by saying, "love the Lord your God with all your heart, with all your soul, with all your mind, and with all your strength. The second is this: 'You must love your neighbour as yourself.' No other commandment is greater than these." Mark 12:20. Note the use of the singular and then plural in describing the commandment in the last sentence.

In all the gospels, the language that Jesus uses implies that he found it difficult to speak of the two commandments as being separate (especially so in Luke 10:27). He seemed to see the boundaries between them as being very indistinct and that the one should not be thought of without immediately thinking of the other.

We know that we really ought to regard them as one commandment because we cannot love God without also loving our neighbour. The fact that we tend to see them as two is evidence of the separation that we have made between being and doing that I mentioned earlier. How else is it that when we think about loving God, it is prayer, devotion and worship that come to mind whilst loving our neighbour is put into the category of doing? Acts of devotion and the expression of our love for God through things like prayer we think of as coming from our being, whereas loving our neighbour has become synonymous with good deeds.

In merging the two into one commandment, Jesus also merges together the two spheres of life that we keep separate. Love for God necessarily entails expressions of that love, i.e. serving him by loving one's neighbour. So the act of service, when performed out of love for God, in point of fact becomes an act of devotion to God.

*****

If you take this principle of loving God through what you do and then apply it to your whole life, *all* of life becomes one act of devotion to God. In Jesus, being and doing become one.

Understand this, embrace it, and let it blow away the kind of thinking that restricts God to just one sphere of your life, and you will take the first steps into knowing the presence of God with you always, but this just the beginning of a life devoted to The Nearest; there's more, and it is even more wonderful.

When Jesus died, we read that the veil in front of the Holy of Holies was torn in two. The implication is that now the presence of God is released from the confines of the temple, and the Holy of Holies of God is in the hearts and lives of those who love him.

Prayer is no longer a place you go to away from the rest of life, it no longer requires you to shake off the dust of the world before entering; the proper place for prayer is actually our world.

Whether or not you are conscious of it, God is the Nearest to you in every moment of life. You need only turn the briefest thought to him and he is here, and he is closer even than this.

You may not feel that this is so all of the time, indeed for much of the time God may not even be a part of your thoughts, but if your whole attitude to life is to trust in this fact of God's nearness to you, because of what Jesus has won for you, then all of life becomes sacred. The boundary between sacred and secular dissolves away altogether, and the possibility opens up of life itself becoming your act of devotion to God.

Your life as it is at this very moment, offered to God, is your devotion.

Primarily, devotion is not really an act at all; it is a loving approach to life that sees God as the object of that love. Clearly, it is possible to go through the motions of seemingly devotional acts without there being any sense of devotion present within the person's heart. As an expression of love, devotion comes from within who you are and is not something to be turned on at appropriate times.

Although I may not think about her every second of the day, nevertheless I do love my wife all the time. I do not only love her in the times when I am thinking about or showing her affection. In the same way we may not think about God all the time but we either love God, or we do not. This in turn means that devotion to God is no longer restricted to those acts that explicitly express it.

## Service As Devotion

If we adopt this idea as a model for spirituality there will be those who are bound to ask where our spiritual sustenance will come from. After all, we are used to thinking of prayer times as a kind of mealtime, feeding our spirituality and giving us the nourishment we need to grow in God.

We can look to Jesus again.

Jesus said once, "My food is to do the will of him who sent me." (John 4:34). For him, serving God was his source of spiritual nourishment. Rather than being depleted by serving and ministering, his relationship with God was strengthened and fed, perhaps because it was the natural expression of that relationship. Naturally, Jesus got tired and naturally there were times when he needed to be alone with God, but we should not read into this that Jesus is having a quiet-time or taking a retreat to recharge his spirituality.

Jesus' source of spiritual sustenance was God and this sustenance was drawn upon through being who God wanted him to be. Serving God in this way affirmed his own identity with God, because it was the natural expression of who he was. Thus, serving God and being Jesus were one and the same thing, bound together in one continuous relationship with God as a constant source of all spiritual life and strength.

Even though Jesus' relationship with God as the Son of God is unique, his relationship with God as a human being is meant as a model for us. It is that kind of relationship described in the last paragraph, which Jesus came to restore to us as children of God. Romans 8:29 describes Jesus as "... the firstborn among many brothers."

This has enormous implications for us because it means that, as it was for Jesus, so our food is to do the will of God. Our source of spiritual nourishment is to be who God wants us to be and to express what God wants us to be in our way of life. A relationship with God, then, is not something we wear, but something that is an integral part of who we are.

If we look at them this way, prayer and service are not acts that we perform, rather they are the natural expression of who we are within God. As it was for Jesus so our relationship with God and its expression are themselves to be our source of spiritual strength.

One of the lines of the prayer of St Francis says, "It is in giving that we receive." Some have taken this, along with the words of Jesus, "Give, and it will be given to you" (Luke 6:38), and created a gospel of material rewards. In this gospel what Jesus says about giving and receiving is interpreted as meaning, "The more you give away materially, the more prosperous God will make you." However, this takes the words of Jesus out of the whole context of his message about the Kingdom of God.

We need to remember that Jesus was talking to the disciples in the context of the Sermon on the Mount (although in Luke this actually takes place on a plain). What he describes in this teaching is the character of the person who will inherit the Kingdom of God.

Those in the Kingdom, Jesus says immediately prior to this saying, are the kind of people who love their enemies and turn the other cheek. They are not judgemental but forgiving and generous. "Give, and it will given to you" must be read alongside the other teaching in the Sermon on the Mount about the poor being blessed and the rich receiving woe.

Similarly, when St Francis says, "It is in giving that we receive," we have to remember that he had taken very strict vows of poverty. He had absolutely no material wealth that he could give away. Likewise, when Jesus sends the apostles out on their first mission he specifically tells them to take no money with them at all.

We see examples of how the disciples continued to live this out in Acts. A lame beggar asks for alms and Peter says to him, "Silver and Gold I do not have, but what I have I give you. In the name of Jesus Christ of Nazareth, walk" (Acts 4:6). They give the love of God, which in that instance meant healing.

Again, in 1 Corinthians 11:23, Paul writes, "For I received from the Lord what I also passed on to you..." and although he is talking about the principle of the Lord's Supper, this is also a general principle for all Christian life. We give what God gives to us.

We receive from the love of God in so many ways, and it is the love of God we give away. It is giving the love of God which is the service of devotion.

This is the ministry of every Christian, whatever their denomination and theological bent, and whatever a Christian gives from the love of God and from within themselves is not only ministry, it is also devotion and, as an act of devotion, it is also a means of sustenance and nourishment in God. This is how St Francis was able say, "It is in giving that we receive." We both give and receive from the love of God because the two acts are not really two at all, they are one. They are the greatest single act we can do.

So we come back to Jesus' saying, "My food is to do the will of him who sent me." Serving and ministering the love of God is also devotion, and in devotion you receive your spiritual food, your daily bread. Far from draining your spiritual reserves away, the act of serving God's love, as the natural expression of who you are within the love of God, actually helps you draw even more on the resources of God.

What I am talking about here is a model for all of life, not just the Christian bits. True devotion is a life lived in the love of God. He is near to you in all of life, so his love is relevant to every part of your life, not just the Christian bits.

Service and ministry do not just relate to activities that you think of as specifically Christian. They are not just the jobs you do in the life of the church, the mission you take part in, or the acts of charity you make. Service and ministry is everything you do in life from the love of God that touches on the lives of others, from your daily work and conversations to shopping and recreation.

This is not the same as saying that everything you do in life must be somehow Christianised, with a suitable Bible text tacked on to them. It doesn't mean turning every contact into a religious discussion, or every job you do into a Christian job. What it means is spending a lifetime learning how to embody those qualities in the Sermon on the Mount and at the same time learning how to be yourself as the person God wants you to be, conscious of the love and presence of God with you always.

As I said earlier, "Being who God wants you to be" sounds like some trite cliché, but actually it contains a kernel of important truth. You no longer have to assume that God wants you to be completely different to the way you see yourself. At the same time, accepting and being who you are is not an excuse for complacency or ignoring the need for growth in spiritual maturity. What it means is that whilst you recognise that God loves and accepts you as you are, there are areas in your life where you do need to grow and change - unless you think you are perfect.

At every moment and at every step along the way, you must continually affirm to yourself the simple truth that you are loved and accepted by God, completely and utterly, just as you are, and that you must love and serve from who you are at that moment.

To be yourself *is* your calling in Christ.

Whatever else you choose to do or feel called by the Spirit of God to do, whether it is being a nurse, a dustman, a missionary or a minister, the only way you can really be of any use to God is by being that person God made you to be, and that is enough. When you become THAT person then you are truly whole. And this is a lifelong calling and task.

Your devotion through service for Jesus can only flow from and through the person he made you to be, otherwise you will find yourself trying to match up to some artificial ideal of what you think you should be. That may come from a role model of some great person, another Christian you admire or an idealised construct. But you are not another Billy Graham, you are not another St Francis of Assisi; you are YOU. Thank God for that.

It goes without saying that people are very different. We have different tastes in worship just as we have different tastes in clothing, and yet when it comes to devotion we find that it is largely shades of the same thing. I am the first to confess that I find it difficult to approach God on quiet days and retreats that require long sessions of silent prayer. If they can be thought of as a bumblebee drinking long and deep from one flower then my own nature is more butterfly-like. On the quiet-days that I have attended I have felt uncomfortably confined and found my thoughts and prayers flitting one way and another without settling on anything particularly constructive.

I discovered, after some experimentation, that the most helpful and beneficial kind of devotional day is one that will allow me to go through several activities; sometimes sitting praying, sometimes reading, sometimes walking, sometimes even chatting with others, but all the time looking to God. This somehow fills all the little bits and corners of my being in a way that sitting fixed to one spot with a candle in front me just doesn't quite reach (though this is rather a stereotyped view of quiet days and retreats).

As I said earlier, even forms of prayer that are purely silent and contemplative require a particular kind of effort that begins with our initiative to enter a certain frame of mind. Sometimes I can just about hear God telling us that we try so hard praying to get prayer 'right', that we don't actually pray at all. Our devotional efforts can so easily be focussed on the method of prayer instead of the object of prayer, God.

What it comes down to is this: Spirituality is a part of who you are, and the expression of it must be born from that, and this is all taken up within "Being who God wants you to be."

The same goes for those deeds we do that are traditionally thought of as "Christian service;" the various tasks and ministries that we take up in the life of the church and its mission. These too are our source of Daily Bread.

In fact, spirituality and devotion are strengthened and encouraged in particular through these things, because through serving God in this way comes the need to pray. We talk to God most naturally when we are seeking how and who to serve, or preparing to share a Bible study, plan the mission lunch, choose the songs for worship, etc.

It may be that you read that last sentence and find yourself saying that you do not have a place in the life of the Church, but you do. Anything you do in the life of the church that touches on the lives of others is part of your devotional service to God, whether it's washing up cups up after the coffee morning, taking up the collection, making food to share or attending worship. Particularly attending worship because how you see yourself in relation to God and those around you is central to what it means to worship, or you are not worshipping.

Everything you do is brought to God, and so becomes a part of your devotion to him. Once again this devotion through serving can only come from yourself, from within who you are. Just as you cannot pray honestly without being yourself, so you cannot serve honestly without being yourself.

The love of God can only come from you, from who you are before God, but this service and ministry is not to be confined just to Christian duties. With the distinction between secular and sacred removed, it can now be expressed in and through all of life.

As God exists and loves in all of life, so we learn to live within him and to love him in all the life that is peculiarly ours.

Even when the serving and doing are taken away from you, as they can be through illness or other means, you still exist, and you exist with God. His incomparable nearness cannot be escaped. When there is nothing left in you but existence itself, then that is who you are, with God, for the present moment. Your devotion at that moment, as at every moment in your life, is to be who you are, honestly and openly, before God. Nothing more is asked for.

When all things are brought together within God, your being and your doing, your capability and your incapacity, you are where you need to be to receive all that you need for spiritual living. You are in that place where you can say with Jesus, "My food is to do the will of God."

This is the divine purpose for every human being, as it says in Acts, "God did this so that men would seek him and perhaps reach out for him and find him, though he is not far from each one of us. For in him we live and move and have our being" Acts 17:27, 28.

## CHAPTER 8

# THE NEAREST IN THE ORDINARY

Some people enter the Kingdom of God gradually. Over the course of days, weeks, years or even a lifetime, they become progressively more aware of the reality of God in their lives and, inch by inch, move closer to making a commitment to him. Even then, I have met plenty of Christians who cannot pin down a specific deciding moment when they became one.

In a way I envy them, because their lives changed and became increasingly Christ-orientated alongside their growing conviction and commitment to him. I can see how the Spirit of God has gradually percolated through every aspect of their lives, so that they have become aware of the importance God in their work, relationships, leisure, spirituality and so on.

It wasn't like that for me; I had a kind of Damascus Road conversion. I am one those people who can pinpoint the exact instant when I became a Christian. Before that moment I was fervently anti-God, telling my Christian friends how I thought they were wasting their lives away; in the next moment my life was flooded with an awareness of the love and reality of God. This book is not the right place to go into all the details of what happened, it would take up too much space, but what I can tell you is that it was in the house of some friends and I was doing the washing up.

I know that a lot of people will read this and wish that they could have such an encounter, and I really do consider myself blessed to have had that life-changing experience, but it does carry certain disadvantages. For one thing, from that moment I had a huge readjustment to make in my life.

Prior to that moment I was very anti religion and my morals were pretty shaky too. I wasn't quite amoral, but I was pretty close, and I liked to tell myself that that was my philosophy. I had had neither a Christian upbringing nor any kind of induction. Suddenly I had to turn my whole life around to the Christian way of thinking and living, and perhaps the biggest and hardest lesson of all was learning to let God into every aspect of my life and let go of the controls that I wanted to keep for myself.

I encountered God with a tea towel in my hand. In this I do have something in common with the people I talked about at the beginning of this chapter - those who are converted gradually or who grow into the kingdom – we encountered God in normal everyday life. Whilst there are those who are brought into the Kingdom of God through great evangelical rallies, missions and all the other special evangelistic events that we put on, mostly I think God chooses to meet them in their daily lives. That was certainly what he did through Jesus.

Of the few accounts that we have of the calling of the disciples, five happened whilst they were at work. Simon (Peter), Andrew, James and John were called whilst they were fishing or at least working on their nets, and Matthew/Levi whilst he was collecting taxes.

Jesus seems to have preferred to meet people where they were, in the ordinary circumstances of their lives. So we find that people encounter Jesus at a wedding, in their homes, on a mountainside, in busy streets, at mealtimes, by a well, in fact just about anywhere that was a part of everyday life. What is more significant is that these were meaningful, life changing encounters. In fact the number of "conversions" that take place in places of worship in the New Testament is relatively few.

Contrary to what you might think, Jesus didn't do this so that future preachers would have useful illustrations for their sermons. He did it because that was where reality was for those people: in their lives, where everything that they understood and held meaning for them was. He meets them in their world so that they can find new meaning in the ultimate reality of God's love, and through this have the boundaries of their world dissolved into the Kingdom of God.

Now, if this is so for a first encounter with Jesus, then why not for the rest of Christian life? It is true that Jesus also went to the synagogues and the temple to speak to people there, but often these were times of confrontation. Where Jesus frequently made the greatest impact on people was outside of any religious context, and it was these everyday meetings that were the ones that became significant to the individuals he touched.

Yes, Jesus speaks to and meets with us in daily devotions, services, fellowship, retreats, prayer meetings etc, but he also seeks to meet us in the commonplace, in the ordinary, *in life*.

He meets us in the ordinary and makes the ordinary significant. It has to be that way so that he can sustain and relate to us in all of life, not just at times that we set aside to be religious.

In Jesus, God is here, but the question is, how do you find him here if you do not have a quiet-time in the traditional manner? The answer is already beginning to emerge. You look to meet him in life, all of life. The act of simply changing the way we think about where you expect to encounter God means that you are beginning to look in the right place. How often have you failed to recognise someone immediately because you didn't expect to meet them outside of the usual context?

If you think that only place you can have a significant encounter with God is in a time set aside for that purpose, the chances are (burning bushes aside) that will indeed be the only place you will meet him. Once you realise that God is here to meet you in every aspect your life, the door to a deeper and richer relationship with him opens up.

The proper place for the expression of devotion is not some place dislocated from your world or reality; it is your heart and life. All that your life entails, from travelling to work in the car, to going to the supermarket or just doing the washing up, is the Garden in which you walk in the presence of God.

It is here, in the Garden of life, where you can walk and talk with him.

Read that last sentence again and think about the picture that is painted in Genesis of Adam and Eve. As they walked about in their world, they expected to meet God. Indeed so convinced were they that he was tangibly there that they naively thought they could actually hide from him.

Yet, how often do we get up in the morning and go out into the world with the expectation that we will encounter God in all that we do that day?   This is where monasticism has an important message for us to hear.

In the monasteries devotion is a way of life and thus the goal is that the whole of monastic life should become devotion. So, for instance, their work in the garden or kitchen is offered as an act of devotion along with their times of prayer and Mass.

In reality it is physically impossible to think about God every waking moment. Yet you can practice the art of talking to him in the in-between moments; those short instants of time that we find in the car, going out to the coffee machine, walking to the shops or even in the shower or bath – they can all become moments where you briefly turn the focus of your life to God. A moment to thank God that he is with you, a moment to thank him for what measure of health and comfort you have, a moment to offer your love to God through whatever you may be doing, a moment to ask his help or guidance, a moment to lay a thought or concern for someone else before God, and so on. In this way, devotion becomes what you can offer, not what you can't.

But all this is still just a beginning.

Changing the way you approach spirituality involves developing the art of expecting to meet God as you go about your daily lives; it involves cultivating an anticipation of an encounter with God in the supermarket, at work, at a wedding, in the street – in your Here. It is "Practising the Presence", as Brother Lawrence put it, in the broadest possible sense.

With this as a starting point, it is possible to see that the depth of your spirituality is now no longer related to the quantity of prayers that you say, the amount of time spent doing them, or even the way that you say them. Instead, your spirituality is defined by your openness to God and the directing of your lives towards him, which is the way you came to God in the first place.

I think we know this, deep down, it is just that it gets lost or overlaid as we later learn the other practices and teaching about prayer that are intended to help us develop a mature pattern to our devotion. So, in a way, what I am exploring here is not so much a new spirituality, as a return to a simpler, more naïve one.

As you start to develop a spirituality that is rooted in your daily life, the question of how your spirituality is to be fed has not yet been fully addressed. In the quiet-time method, which, as we have seen has parallels with monastic spirituality, there are recognised spiritual meal times. You set the world' aside for while and then, by using the knife and fork of silence or prayer, you feed on the presence of God.

This is perfectly suited to those living a monastic lifestyle as the day is interspersed with regular meals of worship and contemplation. Certainly the main emphasis for the monk is to maximise the amount of time for meditation and prayer in order to be spiritually fed as much as possible. For us non-monastic types, though, this is a bit more difficult to accomplish, there is work to go to, housework to be done, children to be collected from school, friends to meet etc.

The only way for us to be fed is to stuff in all our spiritual food in one main meal for the day, the quiet-time, and hope that it's enough to get us through the day. For years, doctors have been telling how bad this is for our bodies. You risk indigestion or ulcers, and find yourself hungry at the end of the day. It is much better, they say, to have smaller meals more often.

It took me a long time to realise that many of my problems with prayer were to do with digestion. It is almost too obvious to see prayer as your source of spiritual nutrition; feeding on the presence of God, but when you do, it is plainly far healthier to take only as much as is needed for the moment.

So does this mean, then, that you have to use a pattern of prayer similar to Muslims and take shorter, more frequent times of prayer throughout the day? Actually, this is not such a bad idea, although it would still be very much based on the contemplative model of cutting yourself off from the world for a while in order to move into the spiritual realm.

Maybe using eating as an analogy for prayer is not so helpful after all. In fact, I am not sure that there are any direct comparisons in the Bible between the consumption of food and prayer.

Jesus does use food as metaphors and analogies in teaching, and we have already heard him say, "My food is to do the will of him who sent me" (John 4:34). This, as we saw in the last chapter, is opposite to the way we are used to thinking about how prayer and devotion work.

In another food saying, when tempted to turn stones into bread, Jesus said, "man shall not live on bread alone, but on every word that comes from the mouth of God" (Matt 4:4). Here, Jesus is not stressing a need for abstinence from the things with which the world feeds us, he is underlining the supreme importance of dependence upon God for Life.

Just as bread was the staple diet for people in his day, so you should see God as your staple diet. In the same way that you are dependent on food in order to stay alive, so you must see yourself as spiritually dependent on God for the Eternal Life which sustains you now. And in this, it is the attitude of dependence that is important, not the regularity of intake, or lack thereof.

The reason you need to adopt this attitude of utter dependence upon God is because Jesus says he is The Bread of life and that anyone who comes to him will never be hungry again. In other words, when you depend upon him as you depend upon food for life, your spiritual hunger is met completely and you need never look to another source of nourishment again. Like the widow of Zarephath's jar of flour that never ran out, in the first book Kings, Jesus is an unending source of sustenance.

An even more powerful analogy for spirituality is the one I have already talked about in chapter five: the grape vine and its branches. When you use this as your model, you no longer have to think about going to a source of spiritual nourishment in order to get the sustenance you need to get through to the next meal. Instead, your whole attitude is one of reliance and dependence.

In chapter five, I said that in the same way that it is impossible for a vine branch to live disconnected from the vine, so we cannot think ourselves as having some loose link with God. Now we see the reason for this: as a part of the vine, the branch quite naturally receives all sap it needs from the vine. This, Jesus says, is the nature of your relationship with God. To use an illustration from modern life, think of yourself as permanently, intravenously connected to God.

Now we can answer the question of how our spirituality is sustained: the answer is, "By dependence upon the life of the Spirit flowing through you as you live in Christ." A branch on a vine never goes hungry because the sap of the vine is always flowing through it. For the same reason, the branch never has to take a meal because the vine is always sustaining it.

It is not devotions that sustain us; it is the very life of God. All acts of devotion, when we do them, simply affirm this fact, reminding us of rather than renewing our attachment to God.

*****

If you now take this idea and add to it the concept of your life as your Garden of Encounter with God, there is at least one conclusion you should be able to reach. In this alternative approach to spirituality your source of sustenance is God in life, because that is where he is, that is where you meet him and where you find his word to you.

In all your thinking, working and doing, God is here.

Life is there to be fed upon, not passed through or, worse still, escaped from. It is a gift to you; a platter laid with all kinds of foods: suffering, joy, pain, tenderness, frustration, temptation, love... and each one can be a communion bread of the Lord himself.

It is the most wonderful thing of all, that God is not only found in times of quiet reflection and personal devotion, but also in all of life. As I will discuss in chapter ten, this is not the same as saying that God speaks to us or reveals his nature to us through our experiences in life. As I hope to show, this is too limiting. In fact that sort of thinking can be quite dangerous, because it can lead to the what-is-God-trying-to-teach-me-here sort of philosophy, which regards every circumstance of life as being heaven sent for the express purpose of teaching us a lesson.

Quite often the situations you find yourself in are a result of your own (or someone else's) doing, not God's. To blame him for everything that happens to you and look for some divine purpose behind every disaster is tantamount to spiritual fatalism. Instead, what I am saying is that life is your Garden, the meeting place with God, and through the presence of Jesus and his in-dwelling Spirit, he sustains you and communicates his love to you in all of life.

It is not too difficult to look for God and his purposes in life's extremes. His hand on your life is more obvious at the very high and very low points. This is not surprising since quiet-time spirituality is geared towards holding on to God in the desert and meeting him upon the mountaintop. But what about the in-between times? What about the times when life is, for want of a better word, normal?

These are the times when life is neither a wilderness challenge that stirs up your spiritual survival instincts, nor is it a mountaintop celebration that stirs up a great sense of the presence of God. These are the Ordinary Times, and they may be the hardest of all in which to find God and stay close to him, because there appears to be little to stimulate your spirit into action. Yet they have the potential to be the Holiest moments in your life.

Most of life is spent here, in Ordinary Times, not in the desert, which appears to be without end, nor the mountaintop, which is over all too soon. It is here, on the plains and in the undulating countryside of ordinary life, where you most need to know God's presence. So it is for ordinary life that we need to be spiritually prepared the most.

The first step towards a spirituality for the plains is to accept, regardless of what you may feel, that God is as much the Nearest on the fertile plains of ordinary life as he is on the mountaintop or in the desert. Just because life is not being experienced in an extreme might mean that his presence is not felt in the extreme, but this does not change the fact that he is here. He is no less the Nearest in the ordinary as he is the Nearest in the extraordinary.

There is not one single moment or experience of life in which God is absent. Why would he be? He is here, his presence is close and it is this nearness of God that is your daily bread. Your prayer then, should be that you begin to encounter God from moment to moment so that each moment becomes a moment of devotion. It is in this encounter with God in life, in its busy highways and byways, that you are able to find strength as he gives you strength for the moment.

This leads to the next step, which is the need to develop a

"seeing eye" for God. This has absolutely nothing to do with "The All Seeing Eye" of some religions – it is actually just a particular outlook on life. Let me try to explain what I mean.

It is time for me to come clean and confess to being one of those people who got caught up in the craze of Magic Eye pictures. If you're not familiar with them, they were those pictures that, on the surface, appeared to be just random patterns of colour but in which, once you changed your focus of vision, a three-dimensional object appeared.

Before you got the hang of the technique and saw the pictures for yourself, there was always a vaguely paranoid sense of conspiracy when others told you that they could clearly see, for example, an orang-utan playing tennis. Once you got it though, suddenly you could see the real image that lay buried in the abstract.

The seeing eye of spirituality that I am talking about is similar. It is a skill like any other life skill that has to be learned and developed. It is the skill of looking for God in all of life and in all of creation, because he can be encountered there in the same way in which he can be encountered in set times of prayer.

Life creates its pattern, sometimes the pattern has a clear design and meaning, sometimes it just looks like a random mess. The temptation is to look at the surface image, and think there must be reason, a Divine Purpose to it, and you end up learning lessons that God wasn't even teaching. On the other hand change focus, look not for some hidden insight from God, but for God himself and a different picture emerges.

It doesn't always leap out you. As with the 3D pictures, there is a skill in learning to see God and not just the pattern, and it is a skill that can take a lifetime to learn. Sometimes you will only see the vague shape of what he wants to say to you; a blurry outline that is only just enough to go on. At other times, by his grace, there may be crystal clarity and his image or purpose is clear.

Then, when you realise his presence, it puts a whole new perspective on life's picture. You see the picture completely differently to the way it was before. The picture itself is only a surface reality as there is still more to be seen and known. The picture itself has not changed, just our way of looking at it, and God is in the heart of it.

## CHAPTER 9

# THE GRACE OF THE NEAREST

There was something like ten years between writing the previous chapter and starting this one. In 1994 I contracted Chronic Fatigue Syndrome (often called M.E.) and, although my health has been improving gradually, it took a long time before I arrived at the stage where I felt able to write again.

Apart from the extreme fatigue, one of the things the illness does is to steal your ability to think and concentrate. All language skills suddenly require a supreme effort. So, for instance, reading becomes very difficult, because by the time you have finished a paragraph, you cannot quite remember how it started.

Words on a page appear to be just that; words on a page without sense or meaning. In fact, I was completely unable to read anything at all for the first two years of the illness. This had a huge impact on my spirituality and on my understanding of what Christian spirituality is fundamentally all about.

Before the illness, I had the freedom to do the things traditionally associated with being a Christian, but C.F.S. takes that freedom away. Like most freedoms, I confess I took it for granted. As you will have gathered by now, I was not the most dedicated person when it came to daily devotions, but at least I had the freedom to do them, along with all those other things we do as a part of Christian life.

From the very beginning we are taught that there are three foundation blocks upon which the Christian life is built: Bible study, prayer and fellowship. Reading the Bible is the means by which we learn about God and the gospel, prayer is the way in which we communicate with him and through fellowship we are mutually supported and strengthened as we share what God teaches us.

In the normal way of thinking, these three are the means of devotion, worship and spiritual strength. They are, we are told, the water, light and nourishment for our spiritual growth and development, therefore without them there is no growth and little, if any, spirituality.

With this understanding of spirituality, the first two years of my illness posed a huge problem for me. It was precisely those three things that I was completely incapable of performing. I could not read the Bible, I could not pray (because I had no clarity of thought, not because I didn't want to) and I could not get to fellowship of any kind.

In traditional spiritual terms, I had nothing left to offer to God, no means of drawing strength from him, and nothing that would be considered part of a normal Christian life. Every means of expressing devotion and gaining spiritual input had been taken away. The only thing I had left was the simplest of thoughts that God was with me, in whatever state of mind and body I was in, and the hope that he understood that all I could manage was very occasionally to say, "I'm sorry Lord, I can't offer any more than to say I do still love you."

From where I stood (lay) my existence with God was just that, existing with him and nothing more. By a wonderful act of grace God had at least allowed me to know that he was there with me. Yet one big question remained. How do I, in my state of devotional poverty, be all that a Christian is meant to be? How can a person have any kind of spirituality when all its traditional forms have been taken away?

Now, (and it is very important that you understand me here), I am NOT about to tell you that Bible study, prayer and fellowship are irrelevant. In all that I am about to say, I don't want you to get the impression that I think they do not have an important place in our devotion to God. All the same, what I have discovered is something even more fundamental to spirituality than these.

Grace.

Like a house torn down to its foundations, when the whole structure of your Christian life is stripped away, what your relationship with God is built upon becomes clear. And underlying everything is a bottomless foundation of grace.

It is on this that everything else is built and, without a proper understanding of grace and what it means to live in God's grace, we are in danger of basing our relationship with God entirely on what we are able to bring to it.

Before we can begin to understand what grace means for us and our spirituality, we need to be clear about the relationship between faith and grace, because we can easily make the mistake of substituting faith for grace.

Ask a Christian the question, "How are we saved?" and you will invariably get an answer something like, "We are saved by faith in Jesus." From this it seems reasonable to conclude that the Christian life begins with faith – the moment we put our faith in Jesus, we are saved. At least that's the conventional evangelical standpoint.

Faith is also understood as being the vehicle for God's action in our lives. I have heard countless sermons on the importance of having faith that God will answer a particular need, prayer request, or provide the healing or a miracle in order for that prayer to be answered. The chief culprit for this type of theology is what is sometimes called the faith or prosperity gospel. If you have not come across it, it goes something like this: In the teachings of Jesus, we are told that if we have faith as small as a mustard seed, we could tell a mountain to throw itself into the sea. Having faith in Jesus also means that we should do the same sorts of things that Jesus did in terms of miracles and healings because that is what he commanded his followers to do. Jesus also promises his followers that if they will trust him (put their faith in him), he will meet all their needs. Furthermore if they give (their money or the equivalent), they will receive (money or the equivalent) back the same with interest.

The conclusion that we are meant to draw from all this is clear: if you have enough faith, you ought to be able to become a prosperous and miracle-working Christian. Conversely, if you are not performing miracles, or at least not seeing your prayers answered, then either you do not have enough faith or there is some hidden sin in your life.

Although this type of teaching does have something to teach us about our expectations of God and what we think he is capable of in the modern world, I do have one or two reservations, the chief one being that if it only takes faith the size of a mustard seed to move a mountain, my faith must be sub-atomic. In fact I think have invented a new particle in physics: there are atoms, then protons and neutrons, then, getting smaller, there are electrons, and quarks and then, waaaaay down somewhere inside that but even smaller, is the faith-of-Tim-Ross particle.

I do not want to get into a discussion here about whether God does miracles in the modern world. Personally, I leave the miracle working up to God, and believe we should not close the door on any way in which God may want to work in our lives. The point I really want to make is that this idea that our faith is the thing that realizes our prayers and releases miracles from God turns faith into a kind of currency.

I have already discussed in chapter three some circumstances in which it is possible that God, instead of being a person, becomes a kind of prayer and miracle vending machine, only this time the currency is faith. What we are saying, in effect, is if we put enough faith in and press the right buttons (_and only if we do this_), we get what we want out. (Except that this vending machine, being God, sometimes gives you what it thinks is best for you, rather than what you actually want!)

So people say, "If I have enough faith, I can believe God for (trade my faith for) this blessing or that miracle." This sounds fair enough, until you consider that by implication this means that if my prayer requests are not being answered there are, as I said earlier, only two conclusions that I can draw: either I have sinned very badly, so God is not listening to me anymore, or I do not have enough faith... and I have definitely heard _that_ preached from the pulpit.

How often have you found yourself saying something along the lines of, "I wish I had more faith like so-and-so" or "I'm sure I'd be able to do that if only I had more faith"? The moment we say that, we betray the fact that we see faith as something we should have in definable amounts and that it is rewarded with matching amounts of blessings from God, or even with spirituality.

As well as all this, we also look upon faith as a kind of spiritual inner conviction that we need to summon up, in order to get those prayers answered or see those miracles happen. In my mind now, I have a picture of Luke Skywalker in Star Wars straining to raise his spacecraft by use of The Force, and is that not how we sometimes see faith?

Whenever we do this, what we are saying, in effect, is that faith equals belief equals the conviction that we must have in order to make spiritual stuff happen.

The trouble is that a lot of people feel they don't have the conviction, therefore they consider that they do not have the belief and consequently conclude that they have little or no faith. Conversely, ask the same people, "Do you think you could trust in God?" and they are able to answer with at least some degree of certainty.

Quite a lot of teaching about faith is actually more about self conviction than anything else. Often what is implied is that if you can convince yourself enough that your healing or prayer request can happen, it will. The trouble is, there are millions of atheists who already know the power of positive thinking and God and faith don't come into the equation at all.

In all of this the one thing that is missing is grace. We say that we do not believe in salvation by works, but by emphasising faith in this way so much, we put ourselves in danger of making faith another good work.

If I say that I have been saved by (my) faith, then God hasn't saved me at all. I have somehow managed to haul myself into his kingdom through my own trust, belief and inner conviction. We have made faith too active, but when it comes to salvation, prayer, healings, miracles and spirituality, it is not faith that is active, it is God's grace.

In fact faith is far more passive than we are sometimes led to believe. Once you strip everything away from it, what you have underlying it all is trust, just that.

Human beings have been created with the capacity to trust. Just as we can love, so we are able to trust. We exercise this kind of trust every day without thinking. We get up in the morning and turn on a tap, trusting that water will come out. We almost never get up and think: "I wonder if there'll be any water in the tap today? Let's turn it on and find out." Every time you read a newspaper article or watch the news you are taking on trust what is being said. Without some element of trust, there would be no point in buying the paper, you would have to go investigate every single report personally.

That is one level of trust, the most basic level. Another level of trust is that which we place in others to do something that has a bearing on our lives. When you start to think about it, virtually every relationship we share on any level, whether it is with work colleagues, partners or friends, involves some element of trust. This is the simplest kind of trust in relationships of which you are barely aware; like trusting that someone will bring you the cup of coffee they said they would, or will do that task you asked.

There is deeper level of trust we are also capable of that we might call 'intimate trust'. It's the trust you place in someone to keep a secret, or the trust you feel you have with someone with whom you are able to share the more intimate aspects of your life.

This kind of trust is almost like a twin sister to love, growing alongside it as our relationship with a person grows. For any relationship to be healthy, intimate trust and love need to grow alongside each other.

Then there is the kind of trust that we place in something that we cannot see or touch. The kind of trust we show, for instance, by accepting that we are loved when someone tells us that they love us.

So much of what the Bible says about faith makes a lot more sense when you read the word "trust" for the word "faith". This is not to say that they are completely synonymous, there is much more to it than that, but fundamentally faith is about the trust we put in God through Jesus. When you think of it in those terms, you begin to realise that faith is not some thing that can be measured in quantities, which can be stored up or run out of.

When people say, "If I only had more faith..." it makes faith sound like some kind of substance that you can go and get more of, if you could only find the right source. I imagine some faith-impoverished Christian saying to another, "I'm afraid I can't move any mountains today because my faith has run out. I'm hoping to get a bit more at the prayer meeting tonight. Hopefully, I'll be back up to moving a small hillock by tomorrow."

If you go this way and regard faith as a thing that you can possess in amounts, the next step is to conclude that there are things that can happen to you that will reduce the amount of faith you have, until, if enough bad things come your way, you say you have lost your faith altogether.

On the other hand, when you start thinking of faith in terms of trust, you begin to see that you cannot have more trust any more than you can have more love. In the same way that you have love to give, so you have trust. You can trust someone more completely, just as you can love someone more completely, but the bottom line is that you love them or you don't, and you trust them or you don't. As far as the gospel is concerned, it is where you place your trust that is important.

You have been created with the propensity to trust. Through all that Jesus has done, God offers the free gift of a healed, completed relationship founded in his unrestrained love. The apostle Paul makes it clear that this must be a completely free gift, because if it depends in any way upon what we can do to justify such a relationship, we would fall short of the requirements that God would ask of us.

The gift is offered freely, which means that there is not one thing that we can do to earn it, except place our trust in God and what he offers.

Faith doesn't save us, Jesus does; we just have to trust that it is so.

Paul is the one often quoted as preaching a gospel of salvation by faith, and it is certainly true that faith is linked to justification and righteousness in his writings (Romans 1:17, Gal 2:15, 16). If, on the other hand, you try to unlearn everything you have ever been taught about faith being this invisible something-or-other that we have to conjure up, and instead replace it with a simpler, open, receptive trust, his teachings begin to take on a slightly different meaning.

Although, it wouldn't healthy to throw out everything we understand about the faith of convictions, perhaps instead we should talk about trust-faith.

In every instance where Paul talks about righteousness or justification by faith, he is talking about the gift of salvation offered in Jesus. Except, incredibly, the exact phrase "salvation by faith" occurs nowhere in the Bible.

The words "salvation through faith" do appear (2 Timothy 3:15, 1 Peter 1:5), but they convey an entirely different meaning. "Through faith" implies that faith is a passive vessel through which we receive the gift of salvation. "By faith", on the other hand, infers that our faith is the means or method by which we obtain salvation, which lies there like some object waiting for the taking.

But, when it comes to defining exactly what it is that does save us, Paul is absolutely clear:

"For it is by grace you have been saved, through faith – and this is not from yourselves, it is the gift of God – not by works, so that no-one can boast" Ephesians 2:8,9

*****

So why put all the emphasis on faith as trust? Apart from the need to swing the pendulum back a little, there are two reasons. First, the gifts of God's grace, all that Jesus has done for us, can only be received by trust. Second, only through trust can you live by grace.

Just pause for a moment and let that sink in. Let it be one thought you carry with you for a day or two:

Only through trust can you live by grace.

Because of grace we must have trust-faith as without it grace is inaccessible. Does this make faith into another good work? No, because the gifts of grace, like all other gifts, have to be accepted, and ultimately it takes an act of trust to do that.

So, the Gift is offered freely, nothing is required of you in exchange. For your part you just have to receive the Gift and you do that by an act of trust-faith. It must be accepted or else you cannot possess the gift. After all, a gift does not become a gift unless it has been received, until then it is only a potential gift.

If grace is bound by any rules at all, it is only this: Grace first, faith second. The ONLY way that a relationship with God is possible is when he opens the way for that it happen – which is exactly what he has done through Jesus as an act of grace.

God initiates and we respond; it is Grace and faith-trust working together to complete the gift. Just because Grace has made a way for a relationship with God possible, this does not mean that it will necessarily happen, regardless of whether we want it or not. If that were so, we would not have free will and God may as well have made us all into commandment-following, automatically-loving beings, and saved himself and the human race a lot of grief. Free will must exist if grace exists, just as grace exists because we have free will. And because free will and grace exist, faith-trust exists - "It is by faith you have been saved, through grace."

Now read the rest of the opening verses of Ephesians chapter two, verses one to nine. They could almost be a definition of grace. "As for you, you were dead in your transgressions and sins in which you used to live when you followed the ways of this world and of the ruler of the kingdom of the air... Like the rest, we were by nature objects of wrath. But because of his great love for us, God, who is rich in mercy, made us alive with Christ, even when we were dead in transgressions – it is by grace you have been saved. And God raised us up with Christ... in order that... he might show the incomparable riches of his grace... for it is by grace you have been saved, through faith – and this is not from yourselves, it is the gift of God – not by works, so that no-one can boast."

This importance and relevance of grace to the way you think about and express your spirituality cannot be overstated. If your relationship with God is founded on grace then you must continue to live by grace. If you are to live by grace, every action you do that pertains to your relationship with God must be done from the point of view that you live by the grace of God alone. Anything other than this and both your relationship with God and your salvation rest on what you do to achieve them.

Therefore everything you do and every action you take in expressing your love for God must be done knowing that those actions do not themselves create or sustain the relationship, God does. Consequently it is a relationship that is built on the grace of God, not on your actions. The actions you take in fostering your spirituality are expressions of your devotion to God and dependence upon his grace. Anything else and you have a relationship based on reward and merit. And when have you ever thought you could make your relationship with God better by your own merit?

This is not to say that your actions have no bearing on your walk with God. Your actions can easily reject or embrace what God is offering, and either response may stunt or feed your relationship with him. Nonetheless, it begins and then grows by grace.

Grace first, faith second.

Knowing that grace is the foundation of your relationship with God brings you face to face with a truly wonderful and liberating truth. Because of grace, there is nothing you can do that will make God love you more. By implication, and even more wonderfully, this also means that because of grace there is nothing you can do that will make God love you less.

Read that again and let it soak in. Whatever you think the purpose of devotions is, it is not to make God love you more, because that is impossible, he already loves you completely. Equally, the fact that you struggle to have a so-called "meaningful prayer life" will not make God love you less.

Instead of thinking, "I need to do this or that action, or perform this or that spiritual service in order to have a relationship with God." You need to turn the whole thing on its head and say, "By grace I HAVE a relationship with God, and this is how I show it."

Even then, you need to be clear that whilst your actions of devotion stem from the love God has shown you, your relationship with God is not sustained by them, it is sustained by grace.

In Romans chapters five and six Paul talks about being dead to sin but alive to Christ (I suggest you read those chapters now, keeping an eye out for the number of time grace gets mentioned and all the time thinking about receptive trust where faith is mentioned).

The message here is clear; until Christ's saving act we were regarded as dead to God. As far as being able to offer anything towards creating a relationship with God, we were as useful as corpses. So as a pure act of grace, God works in Christ to resurrect us.

Our position now is that we are standing in the grace of God (Romans 5:2). Where we once were slaves to sin, now he says we are slaves to righteousness, which is another way of saying we are slaves to grace; i.e. we are not slaves at all. As long as we entrust our will to the grace of God, we are free - or rather we are bound only by the limits of the love of God.

Can you take grace for granted? Yes, absolutely, it's called sin. Is there a way of dealing this? Yes, absolutely, trust in the grace of God.

Did you notice in Romans 5:20-21 that God's antidote to sin is not forgiveness but grace? Grace makes sin powerless, Paul says, and righteousness is a free gift of grace. Therefore, it follows that there is nothing we owe to sin to pay it off or annul it. As Paul says, "...sin shall not be your master, because you are not under law, but under grace." Romans 6:14. Forgiveness is simply the natural expression of grace.

This leads us on to the next astounding truth which is that being freed from sin's mastery means that we are no longer slaves to any kind of code that says do this or that in order to be right with God. The only correct response to God, once we accept this relationship based on grace, is to love God with all that we have and all that we are, or as Jesus said, "With all your heart and with all your soul and with all your mind and with all your strength" Mark 12:30.

Grace, then, is not just a passive benevolent attitude on God's part towards you. It is something tangible and active, continuously working for you. You do not deserve this, in the sense that there is nothing you can do to earn it. No action you can take will release more grace from God, nor, as I said earlier, can you do anything to stem the flow of grace from God. You simply trust that it is so and respond with your love and devotion.

It seems, in fact, that far from emphasising faith as the supreme good work, Paul was keen to stress the need for an understanding of grace. Have you noticed, for instance, how he begins and ends every one of his letters with greetings and blessings of grace? These are not there as nice Christian versions of "Dear..." and "yours sincerely". Paul wanted to make it clear that all of his teachings and instructions were to be understood in the context of grace.

With his background as a dedicated teacher of Judaism and follower of the Old Testament Law, Paul's encounter with the grace of God was life changing and liberating. It turned his theology completely upside down. You could almost pick at random any passage from the book of Romans to see how he contrasts living under grace with living under the Law (Romans 6:14, for example).

I am convinced that for Paul, grace was the key to understanding the Christian life. As far as he is concerned, it is the only means by which we can be saved (Roman 3:23, 24, Ephesians 2:4-9); it is the continuing means by which we live (Romans 5:2, 1 Corinthians 15:10, 2 Corinthians 9:8); it is our constant source of strength (2 Timothy 2:1, 2 Corinthians 12:9) and it is grace that makes evil impotent (2 Timothy 1:9-10, Romans 5:20, 21)

\*\*\*\*\*

So we come to what I believe are the three foundations of Christian spirituality. These are not actions or services that we perform and say, "Right, I've done that, therefore I have a relationship with God". In truth, they are more about God than about us. They must be, or the Christian life will be built on something we have created, and I don't know about you but I would rather my life was built on the security and strength of God's nature than upon anything shaky I might construct.

As a result these foundations for spirituality are not a guide to what you should do to be devotional, but how you should think. In other the words, they put you in the right mindset so that you can align your whole life with them and put your relationship with God on the right track. They are found in 2 Corinthians 13:14, and they are these: the grace of the Lord Jesus Christ, the love of God and the fellowship of the Holy Spirit.

How many times have you said that at the end of a church service and really thought about what it means? Me neither. It is used so much that has almost become a churchy way of saying, "That's all folks!" but when you unpack the full meaning of this verse you discover a fairly comprehensive description of what it means to be a Christian.

We have begun to see the importance of the grace of God, shown to us in Jesus, which opens the way for us to enter the love of God. This, Paul says, is what it is all about. In his prayer for the church in Ephesus he says:

"And I pray that you, being rooted and established in love, may have power together with all the saints, to grasp how wide and long and high and deep is the love of Christ, and to know this love that surpasses knowledge – that you may be filled to the measure of all the fullness of God." Ephesians 3:17-19.

The whole purpose of Christian spirituality, all the theology and doctrine, everything that has ever been written about Christianity, is summed up in these verses. What Paul is saying, in effect, is that Christianity is not about obeying the rules, it is about exploring the love of God.

This is entirely dependent on two things: the grace of the Lord Jesus Christ and the fellowship of the Holy Spirit.

Equally, "the fellowship of the Holy Spirit" is not just a synonym for "the Church". Whilst the fellowship that we have with each other is a part of it, the fellowship of the Holy Spirit is so much more. It is about the uniting tie that we have with each other and between us and God *in* the Holy Spirit.

Jesus describes this tie in John's gospel as being like the branches of a vine sharing in the life of the vine (John 15:5-9, see also John 14:15-23). It is the life of the Spirit of God that gives us life and unites us with God and with each other. It is a union which can only be received from the grace of the Lord Jesus Christ and which grows out of the love of God.

Ultimately, fellowship is itself a means of grace, because through it you are tied in to the love God. In the Church (capital 'C'), we are united in our common union with God in Christ through the Holy Spirit.

Therefore, whatever else you want to bring to the Christian life, whether it is prayer, periods of quiet retreat, ministry, service, bible study and whatever you think it means to be Christian, your attitude must be that it all springs from the grace of God first. It all exists in and for the purpose of the love of God and only has meaning in the fellowship of the Holy Spirit.

## CHAPTER 10

# THE VOICE OF THE NEAREST

Christians have described the way in which God speaks to us in a host of different ways, some are more helpful than others, but there are a couple of phrases that people use which are, frankly, misleading.

You usually hear the first when circumstances conspire against them achieving a particular goal and it often happens something like this: suppose you lose your job through no fault of your own. After much prayer someone tells you that they've seen the perfect job for you in newspaper. "Wow!" you think, "that was a quick answer to prayer." So, you get in the car to go the newsagent, but it won't start – the battery's flat. "Praise the Lord." You say, "I need the exercise."

When you eventually get to the newsagent you find it's closed because they've had a break-in and the police aren't letting anybody in until Scenes of Crime have dusted it for prints. "Never mind," you think, "This is just a minor obstacle that must be overcome for me to achieve my goal."

You move on to the petrol station, and that's when you discover that they didn't get that day's paper delivery. With some quick thinking you hop on the next bus to get to town with the hope of finding a paper there, however the bus breaks down and by the time the replacement arrives all the shops have closed.

Then, to cap it all, you meet a fellow Christian who thoughtfully spouts the cringe-worthy cliché, "Perhaps God is trying to tell you something." What you really want to say is, "Well why couldn't he have just said it without putting me to all this trouble!" I will come back to the slightly shaky theology behind this phrase later, but first I want to introduce the second misleading phrase, which is its sibling - "God speaks in many ways."

You hear this one spoken by people who are not really convinced that God speaks to us at all. If he does, it would only be in broad general truths that can be understood by looking at creation, or seen in the exemplary life of a saint, or perhaps through a cerebral study of religion. The idea of any kind of personal communication is not entertained at all.

The reason these two sayings are so misleading is that while they both show at least some kind of understanding that God wants to communicate with us, they make us look for his voice in the wrong place – or rather, a place where we can easily (sometimes dangerously) misinterpret what we think he has said.

In the case of the first saying, there is at least an expectation that God wants to speak to us in a way that is meaningful and relevant to us personally. The trouble is, life's circumstances are so complex that we could almost draw any conclusions out of them we want, or don't want.

"Perhaps God is trying to tell you something" puts us in danger of either misinterpreting what he might actually be trying to say to us. "God speaks in many ways", on the other hand, tends to keep God at a comfortable and relatively imper-sonal distance. Close enough to believe that he can give broad general directions about the nature of his character or how we should live our lives, but just far enough that we don't have to worry about him interfering with what we want to do personally.

Looked at from a slightly different perspective, which I will do later, both phrases can actually be helpful. Before doing that, I first want to show you how my own understanding of the voice of God has evolved over the course of my Christian life, but you must promise not to laugh.

Not long after becoming a Christian I found myself sitting at a midweek revival meeting, listening to a stirring message about the need for sacrificial giving as a source of great blessing.

I sat there listening to the urgent need for the Christian to be willing to give away even the last pound in his pocket. I was living on state benefits at the time and it dawned on me that actually I did have my very last pound in my pocket. It was intended to buy the milk and bread I needed until I got my next social security cheque, but the more the preacher went on about "Giving all to God," the more it seemed as if God had greater plans for that pound than mere bread and milk. Somewhere in the town there might be a needy soul for whom this pound could mean the difference between salvation and eternal damnation. How could I possibly hold on to it any longer!

I found a piece of paper and a pen, and wrote a letter beginning something like, "To whom it may concern..." and I continued to tell them of the wonderful love of God in Jesus and by the way this was *the* pound for which they had long been waiting. My only problem now was how to find the person to whom my pound rightfully belonged.

I walked home, note in hand, trying to strike up a conversation with God to get the advice I needed. "OK. God, show me which house I should give my pound to..." As there were a few thousand houses in the town, I thought that this was a reasonable enough request. God could at least narrow the choice down to an estate or, preferably, a single road. There being no immediate answer, I assumed that God was hinting the house must be on my normal route home. I was relieved about this, as it was a mile-long walk without any deviations. I kept the monologue with God going, hoping for the much-needed guidance yet all the time aware that the end of the high street was in sight.

Initially I was hoping for a whole sentence from God (as that day's preacher seemed to get), but as I reached the outskirts of town and the last dozen houses were in sight, I would have been quite happy if he had just blurted out a door number, or written "122" in the shapes in the clouds. Unfortunately, this was not to be.

At last I said, "OK. God, I really need to know which letter-box to put my pound through." It was then that I had the thought, "The last house on the left."

I was quite relieved about this, as I was now only one door away from the last house on the left and there were no houses on the right. I shoved the note through the door, ran the rest of the way back home and for the rest week tried to count myself truly blessed to be sharing in the sufferings of Christ by having dry cornflakes with cream-crackers and jam for my breakfasts.

This little story is my way of admitting the naivety of the first few months of my Christian life. I had had no Christian upbringing and no previous experience of religious jargon so, when people talked about the voice of God, I virtually expected to hear Charlton Heston's voice resounding in my head. After all, when a preacher tells you that God spoke to them and told them to do such-and-such, what else are you supposed to think other than that God really spoke to them?

What actually made me feel as though there really was something significant missing from my walk with God was not so much the people who seemed to be so close to God that they could tell what accent he spoke with, it was the promise of Jesus that I mentioned in an earlier chapter, "My sheep hear my voice."

The way I saw it, I DIDN'T.

I loved God deeply, had completely changed the course of my life to seek him, and could see all through the Bible and the history of Church how clearly God seemed to speak to those who sought him. If the aim of my life were to be a living a prayer to God, then the highest reward for this would be to hear him respond.

It also used to amaze me how distinctly some people managed to hear the voice of the Lord. They gave the impression that they were not only able to hear odd words, like "Go!" or "Pray!" but could actually hear whole sentences, and even have whole conversations with God. What is more, I noticed that God would often speak to them in very familiar tones.

You probably know the sort of thing I mean. You're sitting at the Church fellowship group, the time has come for people to share a testimony of how God has helped them and someone says:

"There I was standing in the supermarket the other day, trying to buy a cabbage for Barry's tea. Now, I was just going to pick one up when something told to stop and pray. You see I really needed some guidance on this, because it was Barry 's birthday and I wanted to get him the best cabbage.

"And as I was standing, looking at the cabbages, and praying, God says to me, 'Edna,' he says, 'you're to buy the third cabbage from the right.' And I said, 'Really Lord, not this one?' And he said, 'Don't be a silly girl, Edna, not that one, the third cabbage from the right.'

"Well, I confess that for a moment, I was in the valley of decision, but I took a step of faith and picked up the third cabbage from the right, and as I left, do you know, I saw that there, on the cabbage that I was going to take in the first place, there was a caterpillar."

I used to have a few problems with these conversations in my early years as a Christian. For one thing, I always wondered why the first word that God said was the person's name. In time, I realised that supermarkets are often busy places and that God could, in theory, be speaking to anyone. I soon realised that potentially it could mess up the great eternal plan, not to mention the whole cabbage economy, if the wrong person heard him say, "I want you to buy the third cabbage from the right." and picked it up by mistake. Who knows what the consequences would be if Barry didn't get the cabbage that God had planned for him from the foundations of the universe.

Secretly, though, I was jealous of those Christians who were able to have these chummy chats with God. It just never happened that way for me. In my mind's eye I imagined that watching these people in their daily devotions would be like listening someone making a telephone call. They would be on their knees praying and all I would hear would be a sentence or two followed by a silence that would be broken only by phrases like "Go on, God! Really? Mmm.... well yes, I suppose I should, but what about...? ...OK, OK, I'll do it today!"

In the first months of my Christian life, I tried having these kind conversations, but they were always a bit one-sided. I found that I was able, with a little effort, to drivel on in a chatty sort of way, but in the silences that followed I always ended up imagining what God might be trying to say. Nearly always this was either exactly what I wanted to hear, but quite frequently it was the exact opposite.

Okay. So I'm overstating a stereotype here, but I do so to make a point. Whilst I do firmly believe that God does speak to us, and does so in way that is personally meaningful to us, the business of relating our experience of God in human terms can be taken too far and is dangerously misleading.

On the other side of the voice-of-God coin are all those who firmly believe that the idea of God communicating with us at a personal level is just a metaphor for saying our ways and God's are not totally disconnected. In this way of thinking, the phrase "God speaks" is just a means of attributing to God the human traits of speech and communication in order to make sense of a Divine mystery; our relationship with God. In turn, this is a roundabout way of implying that there is no actual personal communication between God and us, as we understand it.

All of which brings us to some fairly fundamental questions that every Christian ought to ask at some stage. How you answer these questions will determine way you shape your entire Christian life and understanding of prayer:

Does God actually "speak"?

Is hearing God's voice just a fanciful idea or can it have real meaning for us?

What exactly do we mean by "The voice of God"?

To answer these questions properly, we need to go right back to the beginning, to our creation, and to look at the fundamental reason for our being here in the first place. We need to begin, in fact, with the age-old question that all cultures and faiths have asked themselves around the globe. "What are we here for?"

The Christian answer begins in Genesis and is summed up, ultimately, in the life of Jesus. What these show is that God has made us, and to seek God is the highest goal of human existence, because it seeks that for which we have been created.

We are not some kind of curious table decoration that God made one rainy afternoon when he had nothing better to do. Neither are we here solely for our own pleasures and purposes, with God as a mere observer outside the goldfish bowl. Our existence only has true meaning when it is lived in a purposeful relationship with our creator and this relationship is made available to us through Jesus.

To seek God for himself therefore, is the beginning of devotion, because this has the potential to evolve into a God-centred desire and life. This too, is not an end but a journey in itself. As Christians we often desire many things that are good and holy: we might desire to be more disciplined in prayer, to gain a deeper understanding of the Bible, or know more about God. However, the kind of desire that I am talking about evolves out of these spiritual desires to the desire for God himself.

You are probably saying to yourself, "I am not sure I am really as spiritual as that, or that my desires are really that God-centred". Yet I would be willing to bet that you have often found yourself saying, "Lord I really *do* want to know you more. I *do* want to be closer to you and be as you want me to be."

It is precisely these kinds of deep yearnings that are evidence of the longing for God in the depths of your being which seek to be released and fulfilled. They are there as evidence of your reason for existence.

This desire for God is a part of who you are. To put your relationship with God in the terms of a corny cliché that is nevertheless true, "You were made for each other." It is the answer to the age-old question, "What are we here for?" Your deepest longings are whispering the answer to you, "You were made for a relationship with God."

Now, it would be a cruel God who created you for this purpose, who subsequently awakens these desires in you, who does not then make a real and meaningful response to you. To put it more simply, we have been created for a relationship with God and it is self-evident that a relationship is a two-way concern.

By definition, a relationship is two or more parties relating to each other. In the Christian life this is the dialogue of prayer - the communication of your being with God's. In this dialogue it is not too much to expect that God, who urges you to pray and stirs deep longings within you, will also respond in some way.

God does indeed speak.

As a part of our relationship with him, he speaks to us but we need to define a little more clearly what we mean by "the voice of God".

There are, I think, two ways of talking about the voice of God. Both are helpful but both can be taken to misleading extremes. In fact it will be easier to define these two ways by their extremes.

The first is the, "So, God says to me..." way. This is the third-cabbage-from-the-right way I mentioned earlier and, whilst it is a bit simplistic, it does contain a kernel of truth. When taken to its extreme, there are those who make it sound like God really is chatting away in an audible voice all the time. Often what is actually meant is, "I felt that..." or "It seemed that the right thing to do was..." or "Through a combination of events, things people said and my own thoughts as I prayed, it seemed that God was urging me to..."

If this all sounds just like common sense, there is a reason for it. What I am trying to show is that somewhere within us, there is a part of us that really does respond to the whispers of God. It is not always clear. It is not always easy to hear. That voice is so easily confused with wishes and desires, which we want to be confirmed as the will of God, or with religious dogma that has been laid upon us.

That doesn't mean that we cannot trust this voice or that we should not listen for it, just the opposite. Living a devoted life means doing precisely this. It means taking risks with what we believe God is saying to us... and making mistakes, which we will, knowing that the love of God will be completely unwavering, because this is how we grow closer to him.

This is the "still small voice."

Picture a very bright room, like one of those lighting shops you sometime see. It is filled with lights and lamps of every description. There are sparkling crystal chandeliers, gold and silver lamps, brightly coloured globes, flashing disco lights and even twinkling Christmas lights. And then, in a small corner, there is a candle. The only reason you can pick out the gently flickering flame is because you know that is there – otherwise it would invisible.

You have to change the focus of your attention in order to see the candle, but when you do, suddenly it is unmistakable because the quality of its light is somehow different.

This candle in a bright room is perhaps one way of under-standing the voice of God.

This also helps us deal with perhaps-God-is-trying-to-tell-you-something in a more constructive and helpful way. As I indicated at the beginning of this chapter, this idea implies that God speaks to you in some way through the circumstances that you find yourself in. The real problem here is that it involves trying to interpret your circumstances as if they were a code containing a hidden message from The Almighty.

There are so many problematic questions that arise over this way of thinking about the voice of God. Why is it that God mostly speaks to you only when circumstances are going against you? Why are there no messages to be found in a perfectly ordinary day when everything is going fine? How can you be sure that it is God who has given you these circumstances? Also, how are you supposed to tell whether what is happening to you is God's guidance and not an obstacle sent to prevent you from following God's will?

All of this means that if you look to your circumstances to guide you, you might do exactly what he wants, or you may end up doing exactly the opposite.

The truth is, sometimes you get a flat tyre just because you ran over a nail.

The other danger of following the "God is trying to tell you something" theosophy is that you can end up in a spiral of self-condemnation. This is where, when you find yourself in a negative set of circumstances, and there doesn't appear to be any specific guidance coming through about them, you are left with only two other alternatives; either there is some unconfessed sin that you have committed or else you have insufficient faith.

If, on the other hand, the voice of God is a candle in a bright room, everything changes. You are no longer looking to the other lights for a source of illumination, but to the candle. You are no longer trying to see what God has to say _through_ the circumstances, but what he wants to say you _in_ them. It may sound like semantics, but that change from "through" to "in" involves a complete change of perspective as the focus of your attention turns from the situation you find yourself in to God himself.

It can completely change the way you endure times of suffering and difficulty with God, because it changes all the questions you want to ask. If your approach is that God speaks through circumstances, that leads you to ask questions like, "What have I done to deserve this?", "Why is this happening to me?" and "What message is God trying to get across to me by letting me suffer these problems?" These types of questions, as I have already shown, can lead you in directions that are less than helpful.

If you change your viewpoint to look for what God is saying in your situation the question then becomes, "*Where* is God in all this." Now you are no longer looking at your circumstances with the view that God has given them to you for the express purpose of imparting some spiritual lesson to you. Instead, you begin to see that in any circumstances you may face, God can speak to you.

The circumstances may not be a message but God does still have something to say, even if it is just, "I am here. I am with you all the way, rest in me."

As I said earlier, when Jesus says, "My sheep hear my voice", the point here is not about the sheep's hearing ability, it is about their ability to distinguish their shepherd's voice from all the others. They know where their source of guidance is and have learnt to identify and follow only his voice. So this is not a statement from Jesus to the effect that, "Real sheep can hear my voice." It is really a call to learn to listen towards God in every context and distinguish his voice from all the others that call for our attention.

\*\*\*\*\*

Thinking about how God speaks to us through life's circumstances brings us to the second way that people talk about the voice of God. It is one I mentioned at the beginning of this chapter: the "God speaks is many ways" description. Often said by people who don't believe that God speaks to us personally, nevertheless it too can be helpful in understanding the voice of God, when looked at in the right light.

Frequently, the phrase is used as another way of saying that we can see and understand something of God's nature and being through what he has made, through his creation – and this is absolutely true. If the first way shows us the whispers of God in our lives, then creation is a megaphone declaring, among other things, the majesty, mystery, and beauty of God.

This too brings us closer to understanding all the ways in which God speaks with us, but this is not at all the same thing as saying that God may communicate his intent, love, care, plans etc to us personally and individually. If the life of Jesus shows us anything, it shows us that God wants to be more than a remote being and that he wants to be intimately involved in our lives.

And yet "God speaks in many ways" is quite a biblical phrase. It comes, in fact from Hebrews chapter one verse one, "In the past God spoke to our forefathers through the prophets at many times and in various ways." The Bible also talks about how God communicates his character through his creation. Romans chapter one verse twenty says, "For since the creation of the world, God's invisible qualities... have been clearly seen, being understood from what he has made..."

These passages are really talking about how God speaks and shows his nature and character in broad, general ways through creation. So we _should_ consider the works of his fingers, as the psalmist says. Yet we can go further even than this and sometimes hear the voice of The Nearest speaking to us more intimately.

I remember going for a walk by Golitha Falls, once. They are not really a waterfall in the usual sense of the word, with water pouring over a cliff; they are a set of cascades on the River Fowey in Cornwall. The water surges and bubbles over rocks and boulders, and has a deep, swelling power to it. I have seen other waterfalls, some far more spectacular, but standing there at that moment looking at Golitha Falls, my thoughts became filled with thoughts about the love God. It was as though I were looking at the surging power of the river in one moment of its life, which was without beginning or end. That water had been flowing for countless centuries and would continue to flow on into the future beyond the end of my earthly existence. In my mind's eye, I saw myself standing in the middle of this ever-flowing stream, which flowed around, within and through me. And then I saw how endless was the love of God for me, flowing unceasingly and unstoppable from a hidden source deep in the heart God. God had spoken to me.

God speaks in many ways.

And so he does, but more closely and deeply than this phrase is often intended to mean. In precisely the same way that I felt God had touched me at Golitha Falls, so he can speak through the Bible, through fellowship, in the words of a hymn or a sermon, or in a card we receive. The point is, when your life is focussed in the right direction and you are looking at the flame of the candle, it becomes possible for God to communicate with you because all the other lights in the room lose a little of their brightness.

Of course both these ways of describing the voice of God are equally valid, but that is not the end of the matter. God is found in creation but you can also meet him in the same way in all of life, not just in times set aside for prayer, and this means that God can speak to you in all of life. This way of listening through looking has to be practiced, but it is something that should feel natural and unforced, an expression of who you are because God is close and not a spiritual costume that you put on.

Imagine preparing your home to receive a very special guest.

You know the kind of thing I mean. First you spend hours cleaning and dusting, then all the little bits of clutter that accumulate on every available flat surface get hidden away in drawers and cupboards. Finally you put on your best clothes and behaviour. It's not that you are wearing a mask, pretending to be somebody completely different; it's just that the person the guest meets is a sort of sanitised version of who you really are.

If God is a distant, remote God to you, with little or no interest in you personally, there is a real danger of treating him like a VIP. If you regard him as a special guest he is only there to be talked to at these special visiting times. You do not really think about communicating with him other than at those times.

If God is a distant, remote God to you, you also go into tidy mode. Before you pray you feel you have to get yourself in order, tidy away the clutter and put on your best prayer clothing.

If God is a distant, remote God to you, your conversation has no intimacy. It is formal. You may not exactly talk about the weather, but the chances are that there will be a discussion about world affairs or the health of mutual friends.

On the other hand when God is near, when he is intimately close to at all times, you know he doesn't mind the clutter and the unswept corners because he has seen it all before.

I hope you can see by now that you have been created for a unique kind of relationship with God, and that the garden in which this relationship is to flourish is your life and world.

In this garden God is near to you at all times and he may at any time communicate something of himself to you. By this, I do not mean that God will speak to you in every moment, or that every time God speaks to you there will be a burning bush or thunder from heaven. You definitely should not exclude the possibility of God speaking to you through a burning bush, but mostly, the ways in which God will communicate with you will be more subtle. And notice how I used the word "communicate" rather than "talk."

Your life, with its entire minutiae, is where you exist, and it is here that God dwells with you. He is not up on some higher plain that you have to ascend to in order to gain an audience. Therefore, it will be here, in the small and large details of your life that you should expect to meet him and find him speaking to you.

*****

Once there was a man who saw a pot of boiling stew and felt that God was talking to him about an impending judgment on his nation. The same man, sometime later, felt that God was speaking to him through the death of his wife. That man was Ezekiel. Another man heard God speaking to him whilst watching a potter turning clay on a wheel. We know him as the prophet Jeremiah.

A few hundred years later, having watched Jesus die and not knowing what else to do, some of the disciples decide to go out fishing. After a fruitless day's work they suddenly land an extra-ordinary catch and in that instant they become aware of the presence of the divine.

Two more of Jesus' disciples, walking down a road, find themselves involved in a Bible study, the penny does not drop straight away, but afterwards they realise that Jesus had been with them and was speaking to them.

I have talked about how God is the Nearest for the Ordinary and is the Nearest in the Ordinary, what these passages show is how he speaks to us in the Ordinary. Not every boiling pot would have spoken to Ezekiel, not every lump of clay would have spoken to Jeremiah, they just happened to be the way that God chose to communicate at those specific moments in their lives. We, on the other hand, tend to look at the more extreme events in our lives as the times when there might be a message from God. How rarely do we look for him to speak to us in the ordinary details of daily life, and yet that is precisely where he walks with us.

Look at it this way and prayer is no longer a mode you go into, it is a dialogue with God lived through your life. It happens in your thoughts, in spoken words, in actions and in emotions turned towards him. It is a dialogue that can even take place when the circumstances of life leave you searching for a way to pray.

If we limit prayer only to a period of time that you set aside from life, it creates an expectation that his response will only happen during that time of prayer, in the next Bible passage you read or thought you have.

To see prayer instead as this ongoing conversation with God in all of life opens up the possibilities for him to speak in all of life, or rather it helps you to learn this listening attentiveness.

Having said all this I do not want to give the impression that there is now no need for times specially set aside to focus on God. Just as it is important to look for the candle in the bright room, it is just as important sometimes to switch all the other lights off and focus on the candle alone.

So you do read the Bible, share in fellowship, go to worship, offer your service if those means of communion with God are open to you. But now, also knowing the grace of God, you know that your relationship with God does not subsist only in these things. You do them not out of a sense of obligation, but simply because they are opportunities to put yourself in a position where you can listen towards God.

Sometimes, though, God does speak in a voice so clear it cuts through everything and brings your world, for a moment, to a hushed standstill. It has happened to me only once.

At the time I lived in a bed-sit some distance from the Bible College I mentioned in an earlier chapter. Although I struggled to have a quiet-time, I was at least able to pray sometimes as I walked to and from college. The event happened during one of these walks home after the morning lectures. Although I was half praying at the time what followed had nothing to do with the subject of my prayers.

By nature I am one of those awkward so-and-sos who inevitably does the opposite of what I am supposed to do, so I had not been attending the college's own Sunday services, as required, instead I had been going to a local Methodist Church, and was beginning to realise that there was big wide world of Christianity that I had not encountered before. I had found out for instance, that the Methodists used a system of Local Preachers as well as Ordained Clergy to take their services.

As students, we were expected to pray for the principal whilst he was on his preaching tour in America. So it was, on that day, that I found myself walking home from the college, along the main road, with my mind lost in thought and doing my best to add an occasional prayer for the principal. From out of nowhere a clear and audible voice over my right shoulder said, "Start local preaching."

Just that.

The voice was so clear I honestly thought for a moment that one of the students had caught up with me. I stopped in my tracks and half turned around, with the word, "Pardon?" forming in my mind, but in that split second I knew beyond any doubt whose voice it was, and the adrenalin began beating a rhythm in my chest.

God had called me to become a local preacher.

This kind of experience is extremely rare. It will not happen to everyone and it has only happened to me on that one occasion. Oddly it has helped me to understand more clearly what we mean by the voice of God in normal circumstances. Which is just as well, because my calling to become a preacher stands in complete contrast to my subsequent calling to the ordained ministry.

In my calling to ministry, there were none of the little

prompts or confirmations that I have heard others received. There were no sermons that became especially relevant or words of hymns or conversations that struck a chord. There was certainly no bolt of lightning or clear voice, just a kind of nagging awareness, which grew within me over a period of time that being a preacher was just a beginning. It was a calling that I had to test in very human and practical ways by taking exams, going before committees and taking a few discouraging knock-backs here and there.

This time God's calling on my life was just a whisper that had to be explored. And when you think about it that could almost be a definition of devotion – that we spend our life exploring the whispers of God.

# CHAPTER 11

# WALKING WITH THE NEAREST

I hope that by now you are beginning to see that you have been created for a very unique kind of relationship with God, and that by this I mean you have been expressly designed to fulfil this purpose. This relationship will deepen as you gain a clearer understanding of just how intimately close God is to you.

Through Jesus, God is no longer there, but here. He is near, not far, and this should guide the whole way you think about how you relate to him. There now is no need for models of spirituality based on ideas of separation and distance between God and you. There is no need for patterns of prayer that strain to reach out for him or strive to hold on to him, because in Jesus, God is Emmanuel, God with us.

This liberating relationship springs from the love of God, from his deep desire for you, and it is born from the grace of God in Jesus. Other than outright rejection, the only possible response is devotion – the love of a heart, mind, soul and life focussed on the heart of God.

Just as your relationship with God is a gift of grace, so it grows by grace. It follows from this that whatever form your spirituality takes, it must be with the understanding that it doesn't create the relationship; it expresses it and helps sustain it. For that reason you must learn the honesty of being yourself before God, because you can only meet God and offer him genuine devotion if he can meet *you*.

The context for this relationship is life. It may not be paradise but the reality of your life, with all the pains, joys and experiences it encompasses, is the Garden in which you walk with

God. He is present with you in the Garden, always the Nearest to where you are, whether in moments of sublime awareness of his presence, times of despair and struggle, or simply in all that is mundane and ordinary. It's a model of spirituality we might describe as Walking with God in the Garden of Life.

In this model, life and spirituality are not separate spheres, they are interwoven and symbiotic – each one dependent upon the other, feeding each other and reflecting each other. And when you think about living life from this point of view, you are naturally led to acts of devotion, as Paul says,

"And whatever you do, whether in word or deed, do it all in the name of the Lord Jesus, giving thanks to God the Father through him." Colossians 3:17.

This Garden is no perfect Eden. The presence of God is not always clearly evident. His voice does not ring out clearly from all the rest and, because this is so, God does not leave you helpless. He provides all the resources he is able to nurture this relationship and these in turn provide models for shaping spirituality.

There are, for instance, special meeting places.

Whilst God is near and he can meet you at any and every moment, sometimes there are times and places where it is easier to encounter him, learn about him and offer devotion to him.

Among these are the activities more usually regarded as the traditional acts of devotion: reading the Bible, fellowship, worship, prayer and service. As I said in the previous chapter, it is just plain common sense that reading the Bible, worshipping in Church, sharing with fellow Christians or taking part in service and mission will put you in the right mindset at least to think about God – and that is the beginning of devotion.

At the same time, you need to bear in mind that these are only acts of devotion, but they are not necessarily devotion in themselves. As places of encounter with God, they are one part of the way we express our spirituality; but they are not our whole spirituality, or even a substitute for it.

Think of reading the Bible, fellowship, worship, prayer and service as just one meeting place, one single pavilion, in your garden. They are not _the_ garden, just one feature of it.

It's more usual to put the specifically religious expressions of Christian life into two groups: things like fellowship, worship and service, are religious activities shared with others, whilst private prayer and studying the Bible are regarded more as personal acts of devotion. Since the latter are particularly associated with personal devotions, there is a tendency for devotion to get separated off from everything else and be associated _only_ with those two things.

After all, if God speaks to you at a house group, or you feel particularly close to God during worship, why should they not also be considered as a part of your devotion to him? There is no rule that I am aware of which says that devotion only counts when you do it on your own.

By regarding these things as just one part of your total devotion, you release devotion from being confined to set times of personal prayer and Bible study. Join with them all that you share in Christ with fellow Christians, and join all of this to the rest of life which we see as one whole, lived in the presence of God.

Now there is a sense of all-embracing wholeness of a life devoted to God. Prayer, Bible study, fellowship, worship and service all help us to encounter God and nurture our relationship, but are no longer seen as defining spirituality, just an expression of it. Consequently we are not left resourceless when they become difficult or impossible. There is no loss of the presence of God because he does not go anywhere, and what remains is still love and trust in God and his Grace.

"And now these three remain: faith, hope and love.
But the greatest of these is love."
1 Corinthians 13:13

Knowing now that God is with you in all of life and is present at every moment, it is possible to think about a model of devotion which incorporates pauses with God in the in-between moments mentioned in chapter eight.

Because God is always the Nearest, you need only turn your thoughts to him at any moment and he is there. So let that become the Daily Bread of your devotion. In between the moments of busyness that make up your life, practice this skill of pausing to turn your heart and mind to God.

These pauses may be just a brief turning of your thoughts to him throughout the day, to remind yourself of his presence, love and grace; they might the offering of a specific prayer for someone or something; or they may be longer, fuller pauses of worship of God and the offering of self or the moment. In this way devotion ceases to be something that has a beginning and end at a particular part of the day and is transformed, instead, into a life punctuated with commas, full stops and paragraphs of devotion.

Some of these pauses may be to read the Bible, share in the strength of fellowship, or offer what service you are able. These are brought together with all the other moments of sharing with God and become a part of a whole life which consists in walking with the Nearest.

In a way, devotions have tended to be seen as being like a tap that you turn on once, full blast at the beginning of the day in order to give the garden a good soaking. The hope is that if you get it wet enough, it won't dry out too much before the next time.

If, on the other hand, God's love and grace pour out to you continually like the unceasing spring I talked about in chapter five, it makes sense to have a model of devotion which actually reflects that. Now it's possible to see that devotion is actually more like a drip watering system left on and steadily watering us throughout the day.

Better yet, throw the tap analogy away altogether and replace it instead with the wellspring of eternal life that Jesus told the Samaritan woman would never dry up. Now you have an everflowing source from which your devotion flows.

*****

This is just an outline sketch of devotion, which now needs to be filled with colour to create a richer, more vibrant picture, and you might be surprised if I say that one the primary colours in your devotional palette is discipleship.

That word "discipleship" conjures up all kinds of images, most of them to do with living a disciplined, well-ordered, probably self-sacrificing, but above all spiritual life. So, let's get one thing straight right from the start; the disciples were not the most disciplined of people. We see them arguing amongst themselves, falling asleep when Jesus wanted them to pray, expressing doubts, struggling to come to terms with Jesus' teaching and even being accused of a having limited faith – hopefully you won't feel overqualified for the task of being a disciple!

Before I go any further, here is a definition of discipleship that makes a useful starting point. "**Discipleship:** A disciple is one who undertakes the discipline of his/her teacher. Thus, discipleship is about learning what that discipline is, learning how to follow. It is part education, part mentoring, part apprenticeship, but it goes a step beyond it. Disciples not only take in what they are taught and what they learn from being with the teacher, they take it into their core identity, so that it defines who they are." Copyright © 2000 Spiritual.com.au Pty. Ltd.

www.spiritual.com.au/dictionary/dict_d.html, (17<sup>th</sup> March, 2005)

We can extract from this that being a disciple means learning how to follow Jesus by being with him so that it defines who we are; which is also not a bad way of understanding devotion.

Although they were sometimes called "followers," that very word can give the impression that they were just traipsing around behind him with no real sense of direction or purpose other than that it seemed like a good idea at the time (which is how some might see the Christian faith!). As disciples, however, they learned how to define themselves in relation to God by walking *with* Jesus.

For them, walking with Jesus wasn't just a metaphor for sitting under his teaching; they walked with Jesus through the towns, streets and countryside of life. There were times when they were taken to the mountaintop and glimpsed the glory of God, there were times when they sat quietly at his feet absorbing his teaching, but we have to remember that there are whole days or even weeks missing from the life of Jesus in the gospels.

These were the times when nothing extraordinary happened, when they were just travelling from one place to the next, when they were just walking and talking with Jesus as they went about more practical matters of finding food or shelter. These must have been learning experiences too, as they learnt how to be God's people in life, not just in "spiritual moments."

If you adopt discipleship in this sense as a part of your spirituality, you make your picture of devotion richer and more colourful because, if you go back to that definition of discipleship, you define who you are more clearly by being with Jesus and learning to follow him.

That is something which can only be done fully and completely if you take it into every aspect of your life, not just the spiritual parts. You are only able to do this because, to use Jesus' analogy, you are not detached from the vine but permanently grafted in, with the life of God's Spirit flowing through you – which is the next resource that God offers you.

Jesus used the image of a vine and branches to show how closely bound we are into the life of Spirit, but the Old Testament has another image, that of a tree growing beside a river:

"But a blessed is the man who trusts in the Lord, whose confidence is in him. He will be like a tree planted by the water that sends out its roots by the stream. It does not fear when heat comes; its leaves are always green. It has no worries in a year of drought and never fails to produce fruit." Jeremiah 17:7, 8.

It's very similar to the picture given in Psalm 1, which we looked at in chapter five, but this image of God's people as trees is one found again and again in the Old Testament, especially in the Psalms. If you have a moment, read these other passages: Psalm 1, Psalm 52:8, 9 and Psalm 92:12-15.

The last one, from Psalm 92, in particular gives a powerful picture of God's people as trees planted in the courtyards of God. We are no longer seen as a tree planted by a stream, exposed and open to desiccating summer winds, and which may or may not dry up. We are secure within the walls of God's love, planted in the courtyards of God by the unending stream of his Spirit.

I am not very good with houseplants and I know that we would probably have more plants if I gave them a regular watering. The few we have in our house have survived because they belong to a peculiar group of plants that probably come from a unique environment. In their natural surroundings they would have spent most of the time without any rain, dried up and parched, but this would have been interspersed with occasional periods of torrential flooding.

What these tree passages from the Bible show is that you are not a houseplant, potted up and placed in some alien environment in need of a daily watering of devotions to prevent you from wilting. You are a tree, planted by the River of Life; your roots permanently tapped into the life-giving water of the Spirit.

The passage from Jeremiah says that it is the person who "trusts in the Lord" who is like the tree planted by a river. At first glance this sounds like it is qualifying the metaphor by saying that only people with enough faith (or obedience to God's law in Psalm 1) are good enough to be ever-green, waterside trees. But remember, we are talking about the kind of faith discussed in chapter nine, the kind of faith that is our trust placed in God. Jeremiah also uses the word "confidence" sometimes translated as the word "hope", which brings a whole new depth of meaning to trusting in God.

Isaiah uses the word confidence in a passage that wonderfully describes this kind of trusting faith. Isaiah 30:15: "...In returning and rest shall ye be saved; in quietness and in confidence shall be your strength" (King James Version). Other versions, including the New International Version translate this as "quietness and trust."

This too gives a richer understanding of faith as resting trustfully in the arms of God. To get the sense of what this is about picture a big cosy armchair, the most comfortable, luxurious armchair you can imagine. Now picture yourself sitting back in the depths of this chair, letting go of everything and sinking into it. All your muscles relax as you let it take your full weight and you end up simply resting quietly in it – that is faith.

And that kind of faith is a model that you can bring into spirituality where your devotion to God begins and grows as you learn this skill of resting in the Lord. You are already planted by the river of life in the courtyard of God presence, so devotion for you now is this quiet and confident resting in the Lord, drawing upon all the refreshment and nourishment of the Spirit as he flows through you.

To this understanding of God's presence in your life, who through the power of his grace holds you in the arms of his love, you can bring one more thing to complete your devotion; your response.

There can only be one – service.

Not the kind of service given as a payment, and definitely not the kind of servility of a servant doing his duty – Jesus says that he no longer call us servants, but friends (John 15:15). No, it is that kind of service talked about in chapter seven. It is the service of self offered to God, not because he needs your assistance in some way, but because through this self-offering you become open to receive from him all that he has to give to you.

It is nothing less than the complete offering of your poverty to God's riches so that you, and those around you, may be enriched with all the wealth that God offers.

Having read this book, no doubt some will accuse me of making spirituality convenient and point to passages in the Bible that speak of cost and sacrifice involved in following Jesus and being devoted to God.

Make no mistake about it, there certainly is a cost involved, but I think that we sometimes misunderstand precisely what that cost is. So let's look at a couple of the costly discipleship passages to see what is being said:

"If anyone would come after me, he must deny himself and take up his cross daily and follow me." Luke 9:23,
   And
"But small is the gate and narrow is the way that leads to life, and only a few find it." Matthew 7:12.

Other passages in the New Testament talk of persecution, of trials and suffering. Discussing these in detail would take up another book, so let me just say that the first thing you need to realise is that what is being talked about is self-denial, not self-mortification, and they are two very different things.

The sacrifices that God wants you to make are your heart, life and love offered to him. The cost is in recognising that whilst you do have free will, you offer it willingly to God, and that implies making choices where your will conflicts with his.

Any hardship or suffering resulting from following God's will refers specifically to what happens to you in life, it does not mean that your relationship with God should itself be a hardship and a struggle.

There are other passages that speak of the quality of your relationship with God through Jesus.

"If anyone is thirsty let him come to me and drink." John 7:38,
"Whoever drinks of the water I give will never thirst. Indeed, the water I give him will become in him a spring of water welling up to eternal life." John 4: 13,14,
And
"Come to me all you who are weary and burdened, and I will give you rest. Take my yoke upon you and learn from me, for I am gentle and humble in heart, and you will find rest for your souls." Matt 11:28,29.

There may be sacrifice and cost involved in your walk with God, but in all these the love and the presence of God are nearer still as a source of strength and place of refuge. So whilst you walk with God in the garden that is life, your heart and soul are planted in the courtyards of God.

In all of this, God is the Nearest and though the nearness of God is not always felt, it is always assured.

**Circle Books**

Circle is a symbol of infinity and unity. It's part of a growing list of imprints, including o-books.net and zero-books.net.

Circle Books aims to publish books in Christian spirituality that are fresh, accessible, and stimulating.

Our books are available in all good English language bookstores worldwide. If you can't find the book on the shelves, then ask your bookstore to order it for you, quoting the ISBN and title. Or, you can order online—all major online retail sites carry our titles.

To see our list of titles, please view www.Circle-Books.com, growing by 80 titles per year.

Authors can learn more about our proposal process by going to our website and clicking on Your Company > Submissions.

We define Christian spirituality as the relationship between the self and its sense of the transcendent or sacred, which issues in literary and artistic expression, community, social activism, and practices. A wide range of disciplines within the field of religious studies can be called upon, including history, narrative studies, philosophy, theology, sociology, and psychology. Interfaith in approach, Circle Books fosters creative dialogue with non-Christian traditions.

And tune into MySpiritRadio.com for our book review radio show, hosted by June-Elleni Laine, where you can listen to authors discussing their books.

**MySpiritRadio**